The Foundation Center's

Guide To Proposal Writing

Jane C. Geever
Patricia McNeill

THE
FOUNDATION
CENTER

Library of Congress Cataloging-in-Publication Data

Geever, Jane C.
    The Foundation Center's guide to proposal writing /
    Jane C. Geever and Patricia McNeill.
    p.   cm.
    Includes bibliographic references.
    ISBN 0-87954-492-9
    1. Proposal writing for grants—United States—
        Handbooks, manuals, etc.   I. McNeill, Patricia,
        1941- . II. Foundation Center.   III. Title.
        IV. Title: Guide to proposal writing.
HG177.5.U6.G44   1993
658. 15'244—dc 20   93-26638
                                                       CIP

Contents

Preface

For quite some time the Foundation Center has heard from the people we serve through our libraries and publications that they wanted a basic, how-to book with insider advice on proposal writing. To respond to this demand we commissioned Jane C. Geever and Patricia McNeill of the firm, J.C. Geever, Inc., to write this book for us, based on their many years of combined fundraising experience and on interviews conducted with a select group of grantmakers.

We hope this guide to proposal writing proves useful to all of you who are seeking grants, and we would welcome your comments and reactions to it.

We wish to thank the following grantmakers who participated in the interviews and/or who read and took time to comment on parts of the manuscript.

Preface

We also wish to thank the nonprofit organizations who graciously permitted us to use excerpts from their proposals to illustrate the text.

Center for Responsive Politics
Washington, D.C.
Ellen S. Miller, Executive Director

Center to Prevent Handgun
Violence
Washington, D.C.
Hayes Shea, Director of
Development

Children's Aid and Adoption
Society of New Jersey
Hackensack, NJ
Grace Sisto, Executive Director

Christian College Coalition
Washington, D.C.
Rebekah Basinger, National
Director of the Lilly Project for
Fund Raising Effectiveness

East Side House Settlement
Bronx, NY
John A. Sanchez, Executive
Director

Edenwald-Gun Hill
Neighborhood Center
Bronx, NY
Jessie W. Collins, Executive
Director

Family and Children's Services
Elizabeth, NJ
William Webb, Executive Director

Fanwood-Scotch Plains YMCA
Scotch Plains, NJ
John Ciambrone, Executive
Director

Harlem Interfaith Counseling
Service, Inc.
New York, NY
Rev. Frederick E. Dennard,
Executive Director

Institute for Southern Studies
Durham, NC
Isaiah Madison, Executive
Director

Kenmare High School
Jersey City, NJ
Sister Agnes Fox, Administrator

North Carolina Center for
Nonprofits
Raleigh, NC
Jane C. Kendall, President

Reeves-Reed Arboretum
Summit, NJ
Lu W. Rose, Executive Director

Rena-Coa Multi-Service Center
Inc.
New York, NY
Thomas Phillips, Executive
Director

West Side YMCA
New York, NY
Richard Traum, Board Member

Women Office Workers
New York, NY
Joy Hornung, Executive Director

From the Authors

Proposal writing is essential to the fundraising process, but it can be intimidating for the novice. There is nothing worse than staring at a blank piece of paper or computer screen with the sinking feeling that so much is riding on the prose you must create. Yet, if you follow the step-by-step process described in this book, you can create a proposal with a minimum of anxiety.

Take the steps one at a time. You will be successful in writing exciting and compelling proposals, proposals that will capture the interest of foundations and corporations, proposals that will generate grant support for your nonprofit organization.

In preparing this book, we interviewed a cross section of foundation and corporate representatives to find out their current thoughts on what should go into a proposal. While this material reinforces the steps we describe for writing a proposal, it also presents some notable insights into how grantmakers do their work, the challenges facing funders today, and how they are responding. These insights are a distinguishing feature of this book: they show the reality of the fundraising process from the funder's side of the proposal.

The eighteen funding representatives interviewed include a geographic mix of local and national foundations, one community foundation, two company foundations, and one corporation. Some of the funders represented have been in existence for many years. Others are fairly new. All are large enough to have at least one person on staff, and some employ many people.

While the grantmakers interviewed reflect a relatively broad spectrum, it is important to remember that there are more than 33,000 foundations in the United States. The majority of these have no staff and in fact are so small that the few local grants they award each year can be handled by trustees, lawyers, or family members. Therefore, the comments made here do not necessarily apply to all funders, but they do provide an indication of how some of the larger funders operate and how they evaluate the proposals they receive.

A series of questions was designed for the interview sessions in order to elicit views not only on proposal writing but also on the entire funding process. Interviews were conducted in person and via the telephone, following the questionnaire format. Questions were posed as to desired proposal contents, layout, length, and presentation. Funders were asked how proposals captured and kept their attention, what the characteristics of a successful proposal are, and what red flags are raised when they read proposals. They were also asked to discuss follow-up strategies once an agency receives a grant and whether, and how, to resubmit a rejected proposal. They were asked to describe trends they perceived in the funding climate for the 1990s.

Information and quotes gleaned from these interviews are used throughout the text. Appendix A, "What the Funders Have To Say," reflects the substance of the interviews. Here, the reader can find the specific questions asked of each grantmaking representative with some of their responses. The goal in presenting this information is distinctly not to help the reader learn about particular funders but rather to provide a more general sense of grantmakers' perspectives on proposal writing. The funders interviewed have spoken frankly. They have all granted permission to the Foundation Center to use their quotes.

Acknowledgments

We would like to express appreciation to the staff of J.C. Geever, Inc., particularly to Cheryl Austin who helped prepare the manuscript.

Introduction

If you are reading this book, you have probably already decided that foundations should be part of your fundraising strategy. You should be aware that, together, foundations and corporations provide only about 11 to 12 percent of private gift support to nonprofit institutions. Their support, however, can be extremely important in augmenting other forms of support, in permitting major new initiatives, or simply in promoting the mission of your agency.

Foundation giving has increased dramatically in recent years. During the decade of the 1980s, more than 3,000 foundations with assets over $1 million or annual grants budgets of $100,000 or more were created. The assets of the foundation field tripled during the decade both because of these new players and because of the rise in the value of the assets held by existing foundations. By 1992, foundations held combined assets of $162.9 billion and made grants totaling $9.2 billion.

Unfortunately, competition for these grant dollars has also increased. Many nonprofits are being created to deal with new or heightened social needs. Cutbacks in government funding for nonprofit services and activities have meant that many groups that previously relied primarily on government funds are now turning to private sources to support their work.

In comparison with the figures for foundation giving, according to the American Association of Fund-Raising Counsel (AAFRC) Trust for Philanthropy, giving by individuals was almost $102 billion in 1992, eleven times that of foundations. There is money out there. What you need to attract it to your agency is a comprehensive fundraising strategy that includes a variety of sources and approaches. This book focuses on how to create proposals to win foundation and corporate support.

You will want to tell your story clearly, keeping the needs of those you are approaching in mind. You need to recognize the potential for partnership with those you are approaching.

The Proposal Is Part of a Process

The subject of this book is proposal writing. But the proposal does not stand alone. It must be part of a process of planning and of research on, outreach to, and cultivation of potential foundations and corporate donors.

This process is grounded in the conviction that a partnership should develop between the nonprofit and the donor. When you spend a great deal of your time seeking money, it is hard to remember that it can also be difficult to give money away. In fact, the dollars contributed by a foundation or corporation have no value until they are attached to solid programs in the nonprofit sector.

This truly *is* an ideal partnership. The nonprofits have the ideas and the capacity to solve problems, but no dollars with which to implement them. The foundations and corporations have the financial resources but not the other resources needed to create programs. Bring the two together effectively, and the result is a dynamic collaboration. Frequently, the donor is transformed into a stakeholder in the grantee organization, becoming deeply interested and involved in what transpires.

"Don't approach the funder hat in hand. We are looking for partners so that together we can make an impact," states Vincent McGee, executive director of the Aaron Diamond Foundation. Hildy Simmons, vice president of Morgan Guaranty Trust Company, talks about being "...partners. We want to make an effective collegial relationship which will accomplish our mutual goals."

With increasing frequency, funders speak in terms of making an investment in the philanthropic partnership. Eugene Wilson, president of the ARCO Foundation, states this view clearly: "We look at an investment in our community. We think of our funds as a portfolio we manage. We expect similar returns on our investment in nonprofits as does the manager of a portfolio of stocks."

Other funders speak of investing in people. Terry Saario, president of the Northwest Area Foundation, says, "We bank on people." Hildy Simmons, explains, "It's people that succeed, not proposals. We invest in human capital. This is becoming more and more important as the demands become greater."

You need to follow a step-by-step process in the search for private dollars. It takes time and persistence to succeed. After you have written a proposal, it could take as long as a year to obtain the funds needed to carry it out. And even a perfectly written proposal submitted to the right prospect may be rejected for many reasons.

Raising funds is an investment in the future. Your aim should be to build a network of foundation and corporate funders, many of which give small gifts on a fairly steady basis, and a few of which give large, periodic grants. By doggedly pursuing the various steps of the process, each year you can retain most of your regular supporters and strike a balance with the comings and goings of larger donors. The distinctions between support for basic, ongoing operations and special projects are discussed elsewhere in this book. For now, keep in mind that corporate givers and small family foundations tend to be better prospects for annual support than the larger, national foundations.

The recommended process is not a formula to be rigidly adhered to. It is a suggested approach that can be adapted to fit the needs of any nonprofit and the peculiarities of each situation.

Fundraising is an art as well as a science. You must bring your own creativity to it and remain flexible.

An example might help. It is recommended that you attempt to speak with the potential funder prior to submitting your proposal. The purpose of your call is to test your hypothesis gleaned from your research about the potential match between your nonprofit organization and the funder. Board member assistance, if you are fortunate enough to have such contacts, ordinarily would not come into play until a much later stage. But what do you do if a board member indicates that his law partner is chairman of the board of a foundation you plan to approach? He offers to submit the proposal directly to his partner. You could refuse the offer and plod through the next steps, or you could be flexible in this instance, recognizing that your agency's likelihood of being funded by this foundation may have just risen dramatically. Don't be afraid to take the risk.

Recognizing the importance of the process to the success of your agency's quest for funds, let's take a look at each step.

Step One: Positioning your agency to raise funds/ setting funding priorities

In the planning phase, you need to map out all of your agency's priorities whether or not you will seek foundation or corporate grants for them. Ideally these priorities are determined in an annual meeting. The result of the meeting should be a solid consensus on the funding priorities of your organization for the coming year. Before seeking significant private sector support, you need to decide which of your organization's funding priorities will translate into good proposals. These plans or projects are then developed into funding proposals, and they form the basis of your foundation and corporate donor research.

Step Two: Drafting the basic or "master" proposal

You should have at least a rough draft of your proposal in hand before you proceed, so that you can be really clear about what you'll be asking funders to support. In order to develop a "master" proposal, you will need to assemble detailed background information on the project, select the proposal writer, and write the actual components of the document, including the executive summary, statement of need, project description, budget, and organizational information.

Step Three: Packaging the proposal

At this juncture you have laid the groundwork for your application. You have selected the projects that will further the goals of your organization. You have written the master proposal, usually a "special project" proposal, or one of several specific proposal variations.

Now is the time to actually put the document together and get it ready to go out the door. The next step in the process will help you tailor your basic proposal to specific funders' needs. You will need to add a cover letter and, where appropriate, an appendix, paying careful attention to the components of the package and how they are put together.

Step Four: Researching potential funders

You are now ready to identify those sources that are most likely to support your proposal. You will use various criteria for developing your list, including the funders' geographic focus and their demonstrated interest in the type of project for which you are seeking funds. This research process will help you prepare different finished proposal packages depending on the guidelines of specific funders.

Step Five: Contacting and cultivating potential funders

This step saves you unnecessary or untimely submissions. Taking the time to speak with a funder about your organization and your planned proposal submission sets the tone for a potentially supportive future relationship, *if* they show even a glimmer of interest in your project. This step includes judicious use of phone communication, face-to-face meetings, board contacts, and written updates and progress reports. Each form of cultivation is extremely important and has its own place in the fundraising process. Your goal in undertaking this cultivation is to build a relationship with the potential donor. Persistent cultivation keeps your agency's name in front of the foundation or corporation. By helping the funder learn more about your group and its programs, you make it easier for them to come to a positive response on your proposal—or, failing that, to work with you in the future.

This is the point at which you take the plunge and actually submit your proposal to potential funders. For a discussion of this process, see Chapter 11.

Step Six: Responding to the result

No matter what the decision from the foundation or corporate donor, you must assume responsibility for taking the next step. If the response is positive, good follow-up is critical to turning a mere grant into a true partnership.

Unfortunately, even after you have followed all of the steps in the process, statistically the odds are that you will learn via the mail or a phone call that your request was denied. Follow-up is important here, too, either to find out if you might try again at another time or with another proposal or to learn how to improve your chances of getting your proposal funded by others.

1

Positioning Your Agency to Raise Funds / Setting Funding Priorities

Every nonprofit organization needs to raise money. That is a given. Yet some nonprofits believe that their group must look special or be doing something unique before they are in a position to approach foundations and corporate grantmakers for financial support. This assumption is mistaken. If your organization is meeting a valid need, you are more than likely ready to seek foundation or corporate support.

But three elements should already be in place. First, your agency should have a written mission statement. Second, your organization should have completed the process of officially acquiring nonprofit status, or you need to have identified an appropriate fiscal agent to receive the funds on your behalf. Finally, you should have credible program or service achievements/statements in support of your mission and designed to meet identified needs.

Mission Statement

When your agency was created, the founders had a vision of what the organization would accomplish. The mission statement is the written summary of that vision. It is the global statement from which all of your nonprofit's programs and services flow. Such a statement enables you to convey the excitement of the purpose of your nonprofit, especially to a potential funder who has not previously heard of your work. Of course, to procure a grant, the foundation or corporation must agree that the needs being addressed are important ones.

Acquiring Nonprofit Status

The agency should be incorporated in the state in which you do business. In most states this means that you create bylaws and have a board of directors. It is easy to create a board by asking your close friends and family members to serve. A more effective board, though, will consist of individuals who care about the cause and are willing to work to help your organization achieve its goals. They will attend board meetings, using their best decision-making skills to build for success. They will actively serve on committees. They will support your agency financially and help to raise funds on its behalf. Potential funders will look for this kind of board involvement.

In the process of establishing your nonprofit agency, you will need to obtain a designation from the federal Internal Revenue Service that allows your organization to receive tax-deductible gifts. This designation is known as 501(c)(3) status. A lawyer normally handles this filing for you, and it can take up to eighteen months to obtain this designation. Legal counsel can be expensive. However, some lawyers are willing to provide free help or assistance at minimal cost to organizations seeking 501(c)(3) status from the IRS.

Once your nonprofit has gone through the filing process, you can accept tax-deductible gifts. If you do not have 501(c)(3) status and are not planning to file for it in the near future, you can still raise funds. You will need to find another nonprofit with the appropriate IRS designation willing to act as a fiscal agent for grants received by your agency. How does this work? Primary contact will be between your organization and the funder. The second agency, however, agrees to be responsible for the funds and financial reporting. The funder will require a formal written statement from the agency serving as fiscal agent. Usually this fiscal agent will charge your organization a fee for this service.

Credible Programs

Potential funders will want to know about programs already in operation. They will invest in your agency's future based on your past achievements. You will use the proposal to inform the funder of your accomplishments, which should also be demonstrable if an on-site visit occurs.

If your organization is brand new or the idea you are proposing is unproven, the course you plan to take must be clear and unambiguous. Your plan must be achievable and exciting. The expertise of those involved must be relevant. Factors such as these must take the place of a track record when one does not yet exist. Funders are often willing to take a risk on a new idea, but be certain that you can document the importance of the idea and the solidity of the plan.

Like people, foundations have different levels of tolerance for risk. Some will invest in an unknown organization because the proposed project looks particularly innovative. Most, however, want assurance that their money is going to an agency with strong leaders who have proven themselves capable of implementing the project described in the proposal.

What really makes the difference to the potential funder is that your nonprofit organization has a sense of direction and is implementing, or has concrete plans to implement, programs that matter in our society. You have to be able to visualize exciting programs and to articulate them via your proposal. Once you've got these three elements in place, you're ready to raise money from foundations and corporations!

Setting Funding Priorities

Once your organization has completed the preliminary steps described previously, the next step of the preproposal process is determining the priorities of your organization. Only after you do that can you select the right project or goals to turn into a proposal.

Your Priorities

There is one rule in this process: You must start with your organization's needs, and then seek funders that will want to help with them. Don't start with a foundation's priorities and try to craft a project to fit them. Chasing the grant dollar makes little sense from the perspectives of fundraising, program design, or agency development.

When you develop a program tailored to suit a donor, you end up with a project that is critically flawed. First, in all likelihood the project will be funded only partially by the grant you receive. Your organization is faced with the dilemma of how to fund the rest of it. Further, it may be hard to manage the project alongside your other activities without distorting them. Frequently, scarce staff time and scarcer operating funds may have to be diverted from the priorities you have already established. At worst, the project may conflict with your mission statement.

Start With A Planning Session

A planning session is an excellent way to identify the priorities for which you will seek foundation grants and to obtain agency-wide consensus on them. Key board members, volunteers, and critical staff, if your agency has staff, should come together for a several-hour discussion. Such a meeting will normally occur when the budget for the coming fiscal year is being developed. In any case, it cannot be undertaken until the overall plan and priorities for your organization are established.

The agenda for the planning session is simple. With your organization's needs and program directions clearly established, determine which programs, needs, or activities can be developed in proposal form for submission to potential funders.

Apply Fundability Criteria

Before moving ahead with the design of project proposals, test them against a few key criteria:

1. The money cannot be needed too quickly. It takes time for funders to make a decision about awarding a grant. If the foundation or corporate grantmaker does not know your agency, a cultivation period will probably be necessary.

    A new program may take several years to be fully funded, unless specific donors have already shown an interest in it. If your new program needs to begin immediately, foundation and corporate donors may not be logical sources to pursue. You should begin with other funding, from individuals, churches, or civic groups, from earned income or from your own operating budget, or else delay the start-up until funding can be secured from a foundation or corporate grantmaker.

    A project that is already in operation and has received foundation and corporate support stands a better chance of attracting additional funders within a few months of application. Given your track record, a new funder will find it easy to determine that your nonprofit will deliver results.

2. Specific projects tend to be of greater interest to most foundation and corporate funders than are general operating requests. This fundraising fact of life can be very frustrating for nonprofits that need dollars to keep their doors open and their basic programs and services intact. There is no doubt, though, that it is easier for the foundation and corporate funder to make a grant for a specific project. The trustees of the foundation or corporate grantmaker will be able to see precisely where the money is going. The success of their investment can be more readily assessed.

    Keep in mind concerns of the foundation and corporate funders around this question when considering proposals that you will develop for them. You may have to interpret the work of your organization according to its specific functions. For example, one nonprofit agency uses volunteers to advocate in the courts on behalf of children in the foster care system. Its goal is to bring about a permanent solution to the children's situations. When this agency first secured grants from foundations and corporations, it did so for general support of its program. Finding their supporters reluctant to continue providing general support once the program was launched, staff learned to translate the agency's programs so that now they indirectly obtain general purpose support through a myriad of specific projects such as volunteer recruitment, volunteer training, and advocacy, thus making it easier for donors to continue funding them.

Some foundations do give general operating support. You will use the printed directories, annual reports, the foundations' own 990-PFs, and other resources described elsewhere in this book to target those that are true candidates for operating and annual support requests if you find that your funding priorities cannot be packaged into projects. Alternatively, your general operating dollars *may* have to come from nonfoundation sources.

3. Support from individual donors and government agencies may be better sources for some of the priorities you are seeking to fund. Moreover, having a diverse base of funding support is beneficial for the financial well-being of your nonprofit agency. Foundation and corporation support usually should be coupled with support from individuals donated in the form of personal gifts raised via face-to-face solicitation, special events, and direct mail and/or by earned income in the form of fees or dues.

You know the priorities of your organization. You have determined which ones should be developed for submission to foundations and corporations in the form of a proposal. You are now ready to move on to the proposal-writing step.

2

Developing the Master Proposal: Preparation, Tips on Writing, Overview of Components

One advantage of preparing the master proposal before you approach any funders is that all of the details will have been worked out. You will have the answers to just about any question posed to you about this project.

Another advantage is that usually you will need to customize only the cover letter, to reflect the connection between your agency and that particular funder or to take note of their specific program priorities. Few funders require a separate application form or special format.

Gathering Background Information

The first thing you will need to do in writing the master proposal is to gather the documentation for it. You will require background documentation in three areas: concept, program, and finance.

If all of this information is not readily available to you, determine who will help you gather each type of information. If you are part of a small nonprofit with no staff, a knowledgeable board member will be the logical choice. If you are in a larger agency, there should be program and financial support staff who can help you. Once you know with whom to talk, identify the questions to ask.

This data-gathering process makes the actual writing much easier. And by focusing once again on mission and available resources, it also helps key people within your agency seriously consider the project's value to the organization.

Concept

It is important that you have a good sense of how the project fits into the philosophy and mission of your agency. The need that the proposal is addressing must also be documented. These concepts must be well articulated in the proposal. Funders want to know that a project reinforces the overall direction of an organization, and they may need to be convinced that the case for the project is compelling. You should collect background data on your organization and on the need to be addressed so that your arguments are well documented.

Program

Here is a check list of the program information you require:

- the nature of the project and how it will be conducted;

- the timetable for the project;

- the anticipated outcomes and how best to evaluate the results; and

- staffing needs, including deployment of existing staff and new hires.

Financials

You will not be able to pin down all of the expenses associated with the project until the program details and timing have been worked out. Thus, the main financial data gathering takes place after the narrative part of the master proposal has been written. However, at this stage you do need to sketch out the broad outlines of the budget to be sure that the costs are in reasonable proportion to the outcomes you anticipate. If it appears that the costs will be prohibitive, even with a foundation grant, you should then scale back your plans or adjust them to remove the least cost-effective expenditures.

Deciding Who Will Write the Proposal

While gathering data, you can make the decision about who will actually write the document. You may decide to ask someone else to draft it for you. This is a tough decision. If the obvious staff member you identify to write the first draft will have to put aside some other major task, it might not be cost-effective for the agency, and you might consider whether anyone else on staff could be a skilled writer or a willing learner. Can this person be freed up from routine assignments?

If you lack a staff member with the skills and time to take on the task, a volunteer or board member might be an excellent alternative. You will need to identify someone who knows the agency and writes well. You will spend substantial time with this person, helping to describe the kind of document you want. In the long run, this can be time well spent, because you now have identified a willing and skilled volunteer proposal writer.

If you have found your writer on staff or among your volunteer ranks, you are all set. The information for the proposal has been gathered, and work can commence. Should you fail to find someone this way, then an outsider will be needed. Bear in mind, before you choose this option, that the most successful proposals are often "home grown," even if they aren't perfect. A too-slick proposal obviously written by an outsider can be a real turn-off to funders.

On the other hand, while an insider to your agency will always know your organization better than a consultant, an outsider can bring objectivity to the process and may write more easily, especially with the data gathering already complete. Once the decision is made to use a consultant, you will need to make a list of prospective consultants, interview the leading candidates, check references, and make your selection.

You and the consultant will develop a contract that adequately reflects the proposed relationship. This document should include:

- details on the tasks to be performed by the consultant;

- the date when the contract becomes effective and the date of its expiration;

- a cancellation clause that can be exercised by either party within a specific number of days' notice, usually not less than thirty or more than ninety days;

- a statement that the agency owns the resulting proposal;

- information on the fee that the consultant will be paid and when it is to be paid (perhaps tying it to delivery of the product or completion of specified tasks);

- details on reimbursement of out-of-pocket expenses or on an expense advance on which the consultant may draw; and

- a provision for the contract to be signed both by the consultant and by an officer of the nonprofit.

If possible, your nonprofit organization should use legal counsel in developing the contract. At a minimum an attorney should review the document to see that the agency's interests are protected. Seek out pro bono legal assistance. Do not consider oral agreements to be binding on either side. Put everything in writing.

Tips On Writing the Proposal

Regardless of who writes the proposal, grant requests are unique documents. They are unlike any other kind of writing assignment. Here are some tips for the proposal writer.

For many grantseekers, the proposal is the *only* opportunity to communicate with a foundation or corporate donor.

The written document is the one thing that remains with a funder after all the meetings and telephone calls have taken place. It must be self-explanatory. It must reflect the agency's overall image. Your proposal will educate the funder about your project and agency. It will motivate the potential funder to make a gift.

You do need to put as much care into preparing your proposal as you have put into designing the project and as you are planning to put into operating it. You have spent a fair amount of time determining priorities for raising funds and gathering the appropriate information for the proposal. The information you've collected should be thoroughly woven into an integrated whole that dramatically depicts your agency's project for the funder.

There are some basic rules that apply to all writing and a few that are peculiar to proposals for foundations and corporations.

Get Your Thoughts Sorted Out

A proposal must deliver critical ideas quickly and easily. Your writing must be clear if you want others to understand your project and become excited by it. It will be hard to accomplish this if you have not clarified your thoughts in advance.

This means identifying the central point of your proposal. All of your subsequent points should flow easily from it. Once you have clearly thought through the broad concepts of the proposal, you are ready to prepare an outline.

Outline What You Want to Say

You understand the need for the program. You have already gathered the facts about how it will unfold, if funded. You have identified the benchmarks of success and the financial requirements. With this information in hand, outline what should be said and in what order. If you take the time to create this outline, the process of writing will be much easier, and the resulting proposal will be stronger. Rushing to write a document without an outline only leads to frustration, confusion, and a poorly articulated proposal.

Avoid Jargon

Jargon confuses the reader and hampers the reviewer's ability to comprehend your meaning. It impedes your style. It may be viewed as pretentious. With so much at stake in writing a proposal, it makes sense to avoid words (and acronyms) that are not generally known and to select words for their precision.

Be Compelling, But Don't Overstate Your Case

People give to people. While your proposal has to present the facts, it must let the emotion shine through. Personify the issue. Tell your story with examples. Illuminate your vision so that the funder can share it with you. Don't be afraid to humanize the materials once the facts are in place. But never assume that your writing is so compelling as to eliminate the need for programmatic details.

Try to be realistic in the presentation of your case. Take care that in your enthusiasm you do not overstate the need, the projected outcomes, or the basic facts about your organization.

It is dangerous to promise more than you can deliver. The proposal reviewer is sure to raise questions, and the result could be damaged credibility with the funder. Worse, if the proposal is funded, and the results do not live up to the exaggerated expectations, future support is jeopardized.

Keep It Simple

In the old days, fundraisers believed that the longer the document and the more detail it had, the better it was and the more money could be requested. Today, foundation and corporate funders look for concisely presented ideas. Eliminate wordiness. Simply present the key thoughts.

Keep It Generic

As you progress through the fundraising process, you may well approach a number of different potential funders with the same or a similar proposal. Thus, it makes sense to develop a master proposal that, with certain customizing touches, can be submitted to a number of sources. This does not mean that you must have access to fancy word-processing equipment. A clean photocopy of the basic proposal, accompanied by a typewritten cover letter, is acceptable to most funders.

COMPONENTS OF A PROPOSAL

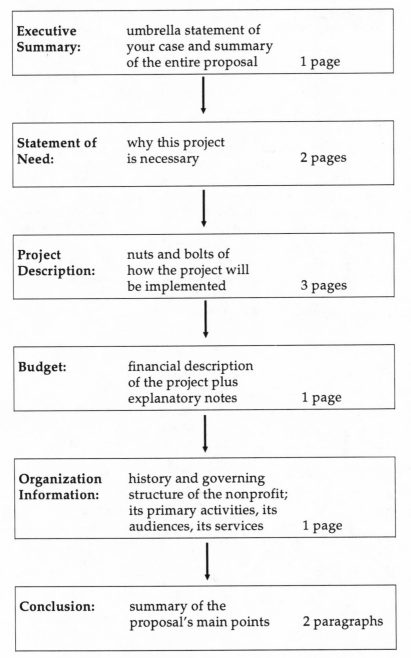

| Executive Summary: | umbrella statement of your case and summary of the entire proposal | 1 page |

| Statement of Need: | why this project is necessary | 2 pages |

| Project Description: | nuts and bolts of how the project will be implemented | 3 pages |

| Budget: | financial description of the project plus explanatory notes | 1 page |

| Organization Information: | history and governing structure of the nonprofit; its primary activities, its audiences, its services | 1 page |

| Conclusion: | summary of the proposal's main points | 2 paragraphs |

Revise and Edit

Once you have completed the proposal, put it away temporarily. Then in a day or two, reread it with detachment and objectivity, if possible. Look for the logic of your arguments. Are there any holes? Move on to analyzing word choices and examining the grammar. Finally, give the document to someone else to read. Select someone with well-honed communication skills and who can point out areas that remain unclear and can raise unanswered questions. Ask for a critical review of the case and of the narrative flow. This last step will be most helpful in closing any gaps, in eliminating jargon, and in heightening the overall impact of the document.

A well-crafted document should result from all these hours of gathering, thinking and sifting, writing and rewriting. Carol Robinson, executive director of the Isaac H. Tuttle Fund, provides us with an ideal to strive for: "To me a proposal is a story. You speak to the reader and tell the reader a story, something you want him/her to visualize, hear, feel. It should have dimension, shape and rhythm and, yes, it should 'sing.' Words are another way to draw a picture, to carve, to create music, to blow glass, to weave, to make porcelain." (private letter, December 30, 1985)

The following chapters of the book include many examples to assist you in better understanding the points being made. A number of these are excerpts from actual proposals and are reprinted with permission from the issuing agency. Please note that to keep the design of the book simple, we did not mimic 8½" X 11" page breaks in presenting these examples.

No two proposals are precisely the same in their execution, and no single proposal is absolutely perfect. In fact, some of the examples presented here have flaws. These examples have been selected to underscore a specific point, but they also illustrate the more general one that flexibility on the part of the proposal writer is essential. In a winning proposal, often the nature of the issues being addressed overrides rules about format.

A sample proposal appears in Appendix B.

3

Developing the Master Proposal: The Executive Summary

This first page of the proposal is the most important section of the entire document. Here you will provide the reader with a snapshot of what is to follow. Specifically, it summarizes all of the key information and is a sales document designed to convince the reader that this project should be considered for support. Be certain to include:

Problem—a brief statement of the problem or need your agency has recognized and is prepared to address (one or two paragraphs);

Solution—a short description of the project, including what will take place and how many people will benefit from the program, how and

where it will operate, for how long, and who will
staff it (one or two paragraphs);

Funding requirements—an explanation of the
amount of grant money required for the project and
what your plans are for funding it in the future (one
paragraph); and

Organization and its expertise—a brief statement of
the name, history, purpose, and activities of your
agency and emphasizing its capacity to carry out
this proposal (one paragraph).

How will the executive summary be used? First in the initial
review of your request, it will enable the funder to determine that
the proposal is within their guidelines. Then it is often forwarded
to other staff or board members to assist in their general review
of the request. If you don't provide a summary, someone at the
funder's office may well do it for you and emphasize the wrong
points.

Here's a tip: It is easier to write the executive summary last.
You will have your arguments and key points well in mind. It
will be concise. Ideally, the summary should be no longer than
one page or 300 words.

Here is an example of an executive summary, taken from a
proposal by the Center for Responsive Politics. This summary
provides an excellent synopsis of the problem and the proposed
solution. It indicates how long the project will take and the
precise cost.

Open Secrets II: The Cash Constituents of Congress

Summary

The role of money in American elections and its impact on the legislative process is a subject hotly de-
bated today, and for good reason. Increasingly, our
system for funding elections makes lawmakers be-
holden to wealthy special interests—political action
committees (PACs) and individuals—who contribute
to campaigns seeking access and influence over the
nation's lawmakers. The U.S. Congress was designed

to be a representative body, responsive to its constituents. It still is. But what is changing, under the current money-dominated system of American politics, is the *identity* of those constituents. With the ever-rising costs of political campaigns, lawmakers are becoming more and more dependent not on their traditional constituents, the voters in their own states and districts, but on a new breed of "cash constituents"— business, industries, labor unions, interest groups and wealthy individuals with an interest in specific legislation and an ample supply of the funds it takes to run a modern campaign. Who are these cash constituents, and where and how do they exert their financial influence?

Open Secrets II: The Cash Constituents of Congress will provide critically-needed answers to those questions. The project will result in the publication of a never before available resource, a comprehensive reference listing of both the PACs *and* and the industry-connected individuals who together supply the great majority of campaign funds to members of Congress. The original *Open Secrets: The Dollar Power of PACs in Congress* revealed the patterns in PAC contributions during the 1988 elections—an important step in measuring special interest money in the U.S. Congress. This new volume takes the process a giant step forward, expanding that data to include all individuals who gave $1,000 or more to congressional candidates. Both groups—PACs and individuals—will be identified and arranged by the industry, labor union, or interest group with which they are connected.

The purpose of this project is to enable voters, journalists, students of Congress, and others to identify at a glance the total picture of campaign funding for members of Congress. The extension of this research to include individuals as well as PACs is essential, since individual contributors account for a major proportion of special-interest gifts to candidates for Congress.

The sheer number of large individual contributions has discouraged serious research into this area, since no organization has been prepared to devote the resources and full-time staff it would take to get the job done. The Federal Election Commission estimates some 400,000 contributions of $500 or more were made in the 1988 elections. Few journalists—or any other researchers for that matter—have seriously sifted through those tens of millions of dollars in individual contributions to determine with which industries and interest groups they are affiliated.

Open Secrets: The Cash Constituents of Congress will do just that, pulling the facts out into the open, just as the original *Open Secrets* brought the patterns of PAC contributions to the surface. In so doing, Open Secrets: The Cash Constituents of Congress will make a profound contribution to a wider public awareness of the real role of special interest money in influencing decisions of the nation's lawmakers.

The project will take 14 months to complete and will cost $212,912.00.

Another example comes from a proposal written specifically for the Lilly Endowment by the Christian College Coalition. In this summary the applicant reminds the funder of previous support and states the problem and the solution with anticipated outcomes.

Executive Summary

Essential to the future of Christian higher education and its impact on our nation is the ability to succeed in fund raising. The quest for philanthropic dollars is intense and for the Christian college, this quest offers some very distinctive challenges. The recently completed planning study funded by Lilly Endowment, Inc., demonstrates that Christian College Coalition institutions need some special help in this vital task.

To address this challenge, the Coalition is proposing a three year, multi-phased project to improve professionalism and fund raising quality and effectiveness. This project will provide a comprehensive program of assessment, training, education and self-help opportunities. These activities will address organizational management, philosophical concerns particular to the Christian college, and management team-building opportunities. Based upon the findings of the planning study, methodologies are outlined within the following pages to provide specific programs for presidents, trustees, development offices and general institutional management. It is the intent of this project to avoid duplication with existing opportunities.

To offer this variety of needed programs while containing the costs within a carefully planned budget, the Coalition proposes to invite experienced administrators and current college personnel to serve as coordinators, workshop and seminar leaders, consultants and mentors. These people will participate as volunteers or for token or part-time fees. To conserve time and travel costs, programs will be scheduled as much as possible in conjunction with existing Christian College Coalition meetings or other conference programs.

Colleges will be assisted in identifying existing programs that address their needs (e.g., CASE NSFRE, AGB, the Center on Philanthropy, etc.). Some subsidy (scholarships) will be available to cover expenses and group rates will be solicited for Coalition members. Additional regional and special topic workshops will be offered at inexpensive sites, and travel expenses for participating college personnel will be subsidized for colleges demonstrating need and approved for travel and scholarship help.

Because of the similarity of purpose of the Coalition colleges, the needs that have been clearly identified through prior research and the strong desire on the part of these institutions to improve, this project should have a significant impact on the professionalism and fund raising effectiveness of these colleges. As a result, they should be strengthened as the following proposal outlines.

Neither example contains every element of the ideal executive summary, but both persuasively present the case for reading further.

4

Developing the Master Proposal: The Statement of Need

If the funder reads beyond the executive summary, you have successfully piqued his or her interest. Your next task is to build on this initial interest in your project by enabling the funder to understand the problem that the project will remedy.

The statement of need will enable the reader to learn more about the issues. It presents the facts and evidence that support the need for the project and establishes that your nonprofit understands the problems and therefore can reasonably address them. The information used to support the case can come from authorities in the field, as well as from your agency's own experience.

You want the need section to be succinct, yet persuasive. Like a good debater, you must assemble all the arguments. Then present them in a logical sequence that will readily convince the reader of their importance. As you marshall your arguments, consider the following six points.

First, decide which facts or statistics best support the project. Be sure the data you present are accurate. There are few things more embarrassing than to have the funder tell you that your information is out of date or incorrect. Information that is too generic or broad will not help you develop a winning argument for your project. Information that does not relate to your organization or the project you are presenting will cause the funder to question the entire proposal. There also should be a balance between the information presented and the scale of the program.

An example might be helpful here. Your nonprofit organization plans to initiate a program for battered women, for which you will seek support from foundations and corporations in your community. You have on hand impressive national statistics. You can also point to an increasing number of local women and their children seeking help. However, local data is limited. Given the scope of the project and the base of potential supporters, you should probably use the more limited local information only. It is far more relevant to the interest of funders close to home. If you were to seek support from more nationally oriented funders, then the broader information would be helpful, supplemented by details on local experience.

Second, give the reader hope. The picture you paint should not be so grim that the solution appears hopeless. The funder will wonder if this investment in a grant would be worth it. Here's an example of a solid statement of need: "Breast cancer kills. But statistics prove that regular check-ups catch most breast cancer in the early stages, reducing the likelihood of death. Hence, a program to encourage preventive check-ups will reduce the risk of death due to breast cancer." Avoid overstatement and overly emotional appeals.

Third, decide if you want to put your project forward as a model. This could expand the base of potential funders, but serving as a model works only for certain types of projects. Don't try to make this argument if it doesn't really fit. Funders may well expect your agency to follow through with a replication plan if you present your project as a model.

If the decision about a model is affirmative, you should document how the problem you are addressing occurs in other communities. Be sure to explain how your solution could be a solution for others as well.

Fourth, determine whether it is reasonable to portray the need as acute. You are asking the funder to pay more attention to your proposal because either the problem you address is worse than others or the solution you propose makes more sense than others. Here is an example of a balanced but weighty statement: "Drug abuse is a national problem. Each day, children all over the country die from drug overdose. In the South Bronx the problem is worse. More children die here than any place else. It is an epidemic. Hence, our drug prevention program is needed more in the South Bronx than in any other part of the city."

Fifth, decide whether you can demonstrate that your program addresses the need differently or better than other projects that preceded it. It is often difficult to describe the need for your project without being critical of the competition. But you must be careful not to do so. Being critical of other nonprofits will not be well received by the funder. It may cause the funder to look more carefully at your own project to see why you felt you had to build your case by demeaning others. The funder may have invested in these other projects or may begin to consider them, now that you have brought them to their attention.

If possible, you should make it clear that you are cognizant of, and on good terms with, others doing work in your field. Keep in mind that today's funders are very interested in collaboration. They may even ask why you are not collaborating with those you view as key competitors. So at the least you need to describe how your work complements, but does not duplicate, the work of others.

Sixth, avoid circular reasoning. In circular reasoning, you present the absence of your solution as the actual problem. Then your solution is offered as the way to solve the problem. For example, the circular reasoning for building a community swimming pool might go like this: "The problem is that we have no pool in our community. Building a pool will solve the problem." A more persuasive case would cite what a pool has meant to a neighboring community, permitting it to offer recreation, exercise, and physical therapy programs. The statement might refer to a survey that underscores the target audience's planned usage of the facility and conclude with the connection between the proposed usage and potential benefits to enhance life in the community.

The statement of need does not have to be long and involved. Short, concise information captures the reader's attention. This is the case in the following example from a proposal by the YMCA of Greater New York:

> **The Need for Out-Patient Housing**
>
> Each year many thousands of people travel to Manhattan for out-patient treatment as hospitals place more and more emphases on ambulatory care. Memorial Sloan-Kettering Cancer Center, for instance, estimates 80,000 out-patient visits annually by people living too far away to return home immediately after treatment. The expense of off-site food and lodging, not covered by insurance, can amount to hundreds of dollars a day for these patients and their family members who want to be with them.
>
> The need is for low-cost housing in a safe and centrally located neighborhood, with a supportive atmosphere similar to that provided for children by Ronald McDonald House.

Conciseness coupled with an appropriate use of statistics are hallmarks of the next example by the Center to Prevent Handgun Violence.

> In 1953 there were fewer than 10 million handguns in America; today there are over 60 million. At the current rate of production—one handgun produced every 20 seconds—there will be 100 million handguns in private hands by the year 2000. Due in large part to their availability, handguns are the instrument in over 22,000 deaths each year. In comparison, more citizens die in handgun fire in just two days in the United

States than in one year in Canada, Great Britain, Japan, Sweden and Australia combined. Hundreds of thousands of other Americans are assaulted or wounded with handguns annually. And over 100,000 handguns are stolen annually from the homes of law-abiding citizens, providing criminals with weapons for further acts of violence. A recent study of the *Journal of the American Medical Association* estimates that gunshot wounds cost the nation $1 billion per year in hospital costs alone.

Most new handgun purchases are prompted by a desire for protection of family or self, but ironically, handguns acquired for self-defense figure prominently in violence. Children are killed or injured because of easy access to loaded handguns at both family and friends' homes. Teenagers commit suicide with the family handgun. Others are murdered or wounded in schoolyards. A recent study by the National Center for Health Statistics, part of the U.S. Department of Health and Human Services, found that one of every ten youngsters who die before the age of 20 is killed by a gun. In addition, an American Academy of Pediatrics' study revealed that gunshot wounds among youth have increased 300 percent in major urban areas since 1986. Equally as tragic, studies have revealed that the people who often place our children at risk of handgun death or injury are children themselves. An estimated 400,000 students brought handguns to school in 1987, including 135,000 who did so daily.

One final example, from a proposal submitted by the Institute for Southern Studies, is a good deal longer than the first two. It combines statistics with suggested actions, building the case for the proposed solution provided by the Institute.

Changes On the Horizon

While some policymakers are reluctant to wade into this controversy, others are concerned about the added burden for family farming posed by the contract system. In the Florida legislature, for example, a member of the agricultural committee is fashioning a bill to give growers the same protections enjoyed by franchise business owners who cannot lose their contracts without due notice and reasonable justification.

Also in Florida, former Congressman Buddy MacKay convinced USDA's Packers and Stockyards Administration officials to intervene on behalf of a grower whose contract was terminated by a major integrator. As a result, the U.S. Justice Department brought suit against the company in December 1989, and a favorable judgment could lead to greater protection for growers engaged in collective action.

In January, a group of growers in Louisiana won a major settlement in their suit against another company that arbitrarily cut them off. Other suits are pending in Alabama and North Carolina, and farmers in several other states have asked the Institute for advice about lawyers, legal precedents or other strategies for correcting the imbalance in the contract system.

Since the release last July of the Institute's report on the poultry industry, we have functioned as an informal clearinghouse for news about these and other developments, including making sure that attorneys have copies of model pleadings and establish contact with other attorneys arguing similar cases. Because many of these cases are settled out-of-court or are not appealed to higher levels, no record of their decisions appears in the standard databases used by lawyers. A new system of communications is required to spread the word, and as we have already seen, the fruits can be significant.

Similarly, the Institute has put farmers in touch with each other and with reporters who have an interest in airing their story. The *Wall Street Journal* article mentioned above directly grew out of our report and contacts provided the reporter over a period of four months. Other reports generated by our study have appeared in the farm and mainstream press throughout the region, giving new impetus for farmers to speak out. The United Farmers Organization (UFO) and Farm Survival Hotline have both received numerous requests for more information from farmers, and we continue to receive calls from all over the region.

Many of the callers say the time is ripe for bringing farmers together to take action on the contract system. Some have already volunteered to act as "key contacts" for an association of poultry growers that would include members in their area. Key organizers for UFO and the Rural Advancement Fund are ready to collaborate and help implement an action plan for building a network that could become an independent organization. And groups like the National Family Farm Coalition and Farmers Legal Action Group have also expressed a keen interest in helping growers organize and focus attention on specific policy reforms for the 1990 federal farm bill, state-level legislation, or innovative legal initiatives.

The Problem

The South's most valuable agricultural product is not tobacco, peanuts or cotton; it's poultry. From the Virginia peninsula to Texas panhandle, an estimated 20,000 farmers are producing 60 million chickens each week under contract for processors who retain ownership of the birds from breeder hen to wholesale delivery. Another 15,000 farmers raise turkeys, breeder hens, and pullets under similar contracts. Census data for 1987 shows that poultry now yields more "cash receipts from farming" than any other commodity in the South. But Agriculture Department officials acknowledge that this $7.3 billion figure measures receipts to the processors, or "integrators," rather than to poultry farmers.

How much did the farmer actually make that year? No one knows.

A 1984 study by and N.C. Agricultural Extension Service found that the typical broiler farmer earned $1,400 per chicken house. More recent evidence suggests that a farmer with two grow-out houses earns less than the equivalent of minimum wage. While the contract system that prevails throughout the industry can provide stability for both processor and grower, it has come under increasing criticism from broiler farmers who see themselves taking larger risks but earning smaller profits.

Under this unique system, farmers borrow heavily to build and continually modernize their poultry houses; they now hold over half the industry's total investment. Processors—who furnish the young birds, feed, and medication—continually seek new growers who can raise poultry cheaper and faster. Since most contracts can be terminated for any reason after each flock, farmers face constant pressure to meet the processor's demands or lose the cash flow needed for the mortgage payments on their poultry houses.

This imbalance between short-term contract protection and long-term debt payments can lead to serious problems. As the attached *Wall Street Journal* article indicates, the system is getting increasingly lopsided as major poultry companies merge, leaving farmers with only one processor in an area to compete for their labor. It is a situation that deserves immediate attention from policymakers and rural economic development advocates. Unfortunately, many legislators, agriculture officials, and trade groups are reluctant to step in for fear of upsetting poultry industry allies. Meanwhile, the contract system itself is being exported by leading processors to hog cattle raising in other regions of the nation.

As you can see from all three examples, the need statement begins the process whereby the organization builds its case and tells its story. This process continues in the next section of the proposal, which describes how the project will address the need.

5

Developing the Master Proposal: The Project Description

In this section, describe the nuts and bolts of the project in a way that gets the funder excited about it, while convincing the reader that you've adopted the right approach. It is worth reminding the funder right up front that your plan is not written in stone. It may change based on feedback from the funder and the experience you gain through implementation. It is not worth putting your organization in a defensive position in negotiating with the funder, and you certainly don't want to surprise the funder in the project's final report when you state that you changed your approach.

This section of your proposal should have four subsections: objectives, methods, staffing/administration, and evaluation. Together objectives and methods dictate staffing and administrative requirements. They then become the focus of the evaluation to assess the results of the project. Taken together, the four sub-sectors present an interlocking picture of the total project.

Objectives

Objectives are the measurable outcomes of the program. They define your methods. Your objectives must be tangible, specific, concrete, measurable, and achievable in a specified time period. Grantseekers often confuse objectives with goals, which are conceptual and more abstract. For the purpose of illustration, here is the goal of a project with a subsidiary objective:

> *Goal*: Our afterschool program will help children read better.
>
> *Objective*: Our afterschool remedial education program will assist fifty children in improving their reading scores by one grade level as demonstrated on standardized reading tests administered after participating in the program for six months.

The goal in this case is abstract: improving reading, while the objective is much more specific. It is achievable in the short term (six months) and measurable (improving fifty children's reading scores by one grade level).

With competition for dollars so great, well-articulated objectives are increasingly critical to a proposal's success.

Using a different example, there are at least four types of objectives:

1. Behavioral—A human action is anticipated.

    Example: Fifty of the seventy children participating will learn to swim.

2. Performance—A specific time frame within which a behavior will occur, at an expected proficiency level, is expected.

    Example: Fifty of the seventy children will learn to swim within six months and will pass a basic swimming

proficiency test administered by a Red
Cross-certified lifeguard.

3. Process—The manner in which something occurs is an
   end in itself.

   Example: We will document the teaching methods
   utilized, identifying those with the greatest success.

4. Product—A tangible item results.

   Example: A manual will be created to be used in
   teaching swimming to this age and proficiency
   group in the future.

In any given proposal, you will find yourself setting forth one
or more of these types of objectives, depending on the nature of
your project. Be certain to present the objectives very clearly.
Make sure that they do not become lost in verbiage and that they
stand out on the page. You might, for example, use numbers,
bullets, or indentations to denote the objectives in the text. Above
all, be realistic in setting objectives. Don't promise what you can't
deliver. Remember, the funder will want to be told in the final
report that the project actually accomplished these objectives.

The example that follows is from Women Office Workers. It is
a brief statement of the proposed project's objectives presented
in paragraph form.

Goals and Objectives

Clearly, Women Office Workers' message "Raises, Rights,
and Respect" has special meaning to office workers who
are over 40. WOW would like to be able to reach out to a
sizable number of older working women, particularly office workers, in New York City to educate them about
their rights and train them to take action on their own behalf. A mutual self-help network will be developed that
will address the isolation of many older working women.
Leaders will be identified and developed among these
women who will promote the self-help networking and
who will act as media spokeswomen to enhance the public image of older working women.

Another example is from a proposal by the North Carolina Center for Nonprofits at its inception on 1990. It is an example of a clear statement of objectives for a project.

II. Proposed Response to These Problems and Needs

The primary objectives of the proposed project are to:

1. Develop a strategic vision for a new North Carolina Center for Nonprofits that will enable it to serve non-profits in the state on a sustained basis;

2. Determine the most pressing needs of nonprofits in each region of North Carolina;

3. Determine what services and supports currently exist in North Carolina to address these needs and what services and supports are still needed;

4. Involve nonprofits across the state in every aspect of the proposed project in order (a) to ensure that their needs and proposed responses are identified from the ground up, and (b) to foster their investment in and support of future activities;

5. Involve leaders from foundations, corporations, and groups that provide services to nonprofits to get their ideas about nonprofits' needs and possible responses;

6. Identify the key leaders in the nonprofit sector in communities across North Carolina; and

7. Begin a comprehensive database of active North Carolina nonprofits. The IRS estimates that up to 35% of the 501(c)(3)s in their records are actually defunct.

Methods

By means of the objectives, you have explained to the funder what will be achieved by the project. The methods section describes the specific activities that will take place to achieve the objectives. It might be helpful to divide our discussion of methods into the following: how, when, and why.

How: This is the detailed description of what will occur from the time the project begins until it is completed. Your methods should match the previously stated objectives. In our example about teaching fifty children to swim, appropriate methods would describe: 1) how the youngsters will be recruited, 2) how they will be taught to enhance their skills, and 3) how their swimming skills will be measured. There would be no reason to describe an extraneous activity like helping the parents learn to enjoy swimming with their children, because using swimming to bring the family together in wholesome exercise is not a stated objective of the project.

The Christian College Coalition in its proposal to the Lilly Endowment presented the action steps so that they clearly support specific objectives. An excerpt follows:

C. Program Description

1. General

a. *Assessment and goal setting.* Each participating college will be requested and assisted in doing an audit of its fundraising program, possibly using the Lilly Endowment, Inc. funded instrument, "Raise More Money for Your Nonprofit Organization: A Guide to Evaluating and Improving Your Fund Raising." Consultants will be made available (if requested or required) through the consultant/mentor network coordinator.

b. *Case statement.* A national task force will be formed to research and develop a compelling case statement on the significant place and role of Christian colleges in our society and in American higher education. Emphasis will be on identifying and communicating the distinctive mission of these institutions with a goal of encouraging financial support. The results of this study will be published for broad distribution in an attractive four-color publication that will complement existing college publications.

c. *Team workshops.* Annual workshops will be conducted for campus teams of presidents, trustees, and development officers. With a specific orientation to fund raising, each team will be assisted to do its own strategic planning, program, design and goal setting.

d. *Consulting/mentor network.* A system will be developed for identifying qualified consultants and mentors among *Christian College Coalition* personnel. Procedures for making them available to individuals and institutions desiring this type of assistance will be developed. A category of needs and areas of expertise will be developed, and a coordination center will be established and maintained for the duration of the project.

e. *Networking existing training resources.* A system will be developed for identifying training resources that exist. A coordinating center will be established to identify existing training programs, to act as liaison with a sponsoring organization, to make the information available to participating colleges and, on some occasions, to develop supplemental programs that will be annexed to existing programs.

f. *Communication.* In addition to regular coverage in the Coalition's monthly newsletter, consideration will be given to developing a regular means of providing information and showcasing exemplary models of programs in the project. Such communication would be designed to provide encouragement and facilitate institutional advancement and project progress.

g. *Scholarships.* Limited financial assistance for upcoming conferences will be made available to encourage attendance at existing conferences that could be very beneficial to presidents, trustees, and development officers who demonstrate need.

Think about how you can most readily construct a logical sequence from each objective to its relevant method. This can be accomplished in a number of ways, some relating simply to visual placement on the page.

One means of organizing this section is to write out each objective and to list beneath it the method(s) that will make the objective possible. It would look like this:

Objective: to recruit seventy children

Methods:

- Put up signs in the Y.
- Go to each school and address classes on the fun of swimming.
- Put ads in the local paper.
- Enclose a flyer about the program with the next mailer sent out to each family in the community.

The methods should match the magnitude of the objectives. Once you are sure that each objective has related methods that describe how the objective will be achieved, you should check that the emphasis given each method matches the importance of the related objective. In our swimming example, recruitment of seventy children is probably the least important objective; demonstrating that fifty of them can pass the Red Cross test is more critical. To match the magnitude of the objectives with appropriate detail about the project, more emphasis should be placed on the testing than on recruiting. (This refining and highlighting of information will enable the reader to understand the project and to have confidence in your agency.)

The methods should appear doable; otherwise, you lose credibility. For example, if the swimming course is to be taught by an Olympic swimmer who remains anonymous, the reader might question whether the organization can deliver what it has promised. However, if the Olympic star is identified by name and has already agreed to run the program, the reader will likely be convinced.

When: The methods section should present the order and timing for the tasks. It might make sense to provide a timetable so that the reader does not have to map out the sequencing on his own. The timetable could look like the one following, taken from the Women Office Workers' proposal. You will note that the timetable is in narrative form. It depicts one year's activities broken down into quarters.

Project Timeline

First Quarter

- Experts in the five subject areas are contracted and scheduled to give one of the five training workshops to committee members.

- At least 8-10 WOW members over the age of 40 take the series of 2-hour training workshops.

- Training sessions are taped, transcribed and summarized for legal rights brochures, one for each topic.

Second Quarter

- Lay advocates begin taking referrals from WOW office for counseling job problems of older working women. Ongoing throughout project.

- Public service announcements are mailed out to radio stations and community organizations announcing the monthly job problems clinics. Monthly clinics begin in this quarter and continue throughout project. Availability of lay advocate speakers on the age issue will be made known to community organizations.

- Follow-up calls will be made to established women's organizations in boroughs and outlying areas of Manhattan in order to begin scheduling public informational meetings.

Third Quarter

- Committee designs leaflet for publicizing lunchtime workshops on sex and age discrimination to be held in the major business districts of Manhattan.

- One lunchtime workshop will be held during this period. Area will be leafletted previous to meeting. Workshop participants will fill out a needs assessment sheet. Follow-up on individual cases will be carried out by lay advocates and staff coordinator.

- Two speaking engagements will be finalized and made in the form of public meetings held outside of Manhattan.

Fourth Quarter

- A second lunchtime workshop will be held in Manhattan.
- Two additional speaking engagements will be finalized and made in the form of public meetings held outside of Manhattan.
- Committee and staff evaluate project; summarize needs assessment sheets and case histories into a brief report that outlines the major problems specific to older women office workers in the New York metropolitan area and the degree of resolution of these problems made as a result of this project.

Another presentation of a good work plan is the one that the Center for Responsive Politics included in its proposal. This plan is divided into phases of work, each with its own timetable.

Phase I: Classification of Individuals. The first step in compiling the data for the new edition of *Open Secrets* is to determine the corporate, labor union or interest group affiliations of the estimated 400,000 individuals giving large contributions in the 1990 elections. The raw materials for the classifications will be the records filed by the candidates with the Federal Election Commission. All contributions of $200 or more are entered into the FEC's computers, along with the city, state, zip code and occupation or employer of the contributor—where that information is available. (Unfortunately, occupation and employer information is often omitted or incomplete when the candidates file their reports, so supplementary research beyond the computer tapes will also be necessary.) Because of the sheer number of contributors, the Center will begin by classifying only those contributions totalling $1,000 or more. If time permits, additional contributions of $500 or more will be examined. In any case, this phase will be the lengthiest and the most research-intensive. This opening phase of the project will take approximately six months.

Phase Two: Updating of PAC Classifications. Modern American corporations are hardly static. Over a two-year period, many corporations divest themselves of old divisions and subsidiaries, or purchase new ones. Companies shift emphasis, move into new fields, or are swallowed by other companies. For all these reasons, the corporations that sponsor PACs need to be reassessed and their industrial categories updated. At the same time, many companies (and ideological groups) are forming new PACs, and these too must be classified. This updating and subsequent reclassification of PAC's will take approximately three months.

Phase Three: Analysis. Once the classifications are complete, the analysis of the patterns in special interest giving can begin. This process will be similar to the analysis undertaken for the original *Open Secrets* project, and the findings will be condensed into charts and narratives in the "Big Picture" section of the book. Because we will be classifying individual as well as PAC contributions, the overall picture of special interest giving will be far more complete than in the first edition of *Open Secrets.* Likewise, it may also be possible to include, for the first time, a chart for each member showing how much money they raised in-state versus out-of-state. This phase will take approximately two months to complete.

Phase Four: Page Design and Layout. Open Secrets will be approximately 1,200 pages in length. Included in this volume will be the contribution profiles of every member of Congress, in both the House and Senate. Layout of the pages, including the generation of more than 2,000 charts and graphs, will take approximately three months.

Phase Five: Publication. Congressional Quarterly Books, which is publishing the first edition of *Open Secrets*, has already expressed interest in publishing *Open Secrets: The Cash Constituents of Congress.* In fact, our contract with them to publish the first edition of *Open Secrets* includes specific language giving CQ the right of first refusal to subsequent editions of the book. They are enthusiastic about the project and will be promoting it accordingly. The time lag from the date of delivery to the publisher to the completion of the final book will be approximately two months.

The timetable tells the reader "when" and provides another summary of the project that supports the rest of the methods section.

Why: You may need to defend your chosen methods, especially if they are new or unorthodox. Why will the planned work lead to the outcomes you anticipate? You can answer this question in a number of ways including using examples of other projects that work and expert testimony.

The methods section enables the reader to visualize the implementation of the project. It should convince the reader that your agency knows what it is doing, thereby establishing credibility.

Staffing/Administration

In describing the methods, you will have mentioned staffing for the project. You now need to devote a few sentences to discussing the number of staff, their qualifications, and specific assignments. Details about individual staff members involved in the project can be included either as part of this section or in the appendix, depending on the length and importance of this information.

"Staffing" may refer to volunteers or to consultants, as well as to paid staff. Most proposal writers do not develop staffing sections for projects that are primarily volunteer run. Describing tasks that volunteers will undertake, however, can be most helpful to the proposal reader. Such information underscores the value added by the volunteers and the cost-effectiveness of the project.

For a project with paid staff, be certain to describe which staff will work full time and which will work part time on the project. Identify staff already employed by your nonprofit and those to be recruited specifically for the project. How will you free up the time of an already fully deployed individual?

Salary and project costs are affected by the qualifications of the staff. Delineate the practical experience you require for key staff, as well as level of expertise and educational background. If an individual has already been selected to direct the program, summarize his or her credentials and include a brief biographical sketch in the appendix. A strong project director can help influence a grant decision.

Explain anything unusual about the proposed staffing for the project. It is better to include such information in the proposal narrative than to have the funder raise questions once the proposal review begins.

Three samples of staffing sections follow. The first is part of a proposal by the Institute for Southern Studies. This example provides the names and qualifications of those who will be involved in the project, including paid staff, collaborators from other organizations, and consulting researchers. It notes the specific aspect of work for which each will be responsible.

Staff Capacity

The project will be supervised by Bob Hall, research director of the Institute for Southern Studies. Hall has been with the Institute since 1970 and has coordinated a number of its projects, including the production of "Ruling the Roost," a major investigation of the poultry industry.

Also deeply involved in planning and implementing the project are Betty Bailey and Mary Clouse of the Rural Advancement Fund's Farm Survival Project, and Benny Bunting, president of the United Farmers Organization and acting president of the National Family Farm Coalition. Both Clouse and Bunting know poultry farming from firsthand experience, and both are already involved in the newsletter, collection of contracts, and building of the growers' network.

For the farmer survey, contract analysis, and policy review, the Institute will draw on the expertise and students of three area faculty members: Drs. John Wilson, Duke University Sociology Department; Michael Schulman, N.C. State Department of Sociology and Anthropology; and Dan Pollitt, UNC Law School. The first two, veteran researchers on the farm family and rural economy, will help develop the survey questionnaires, provide student interviewers, and analyze the survey results. Dr. Pollitt and his law students will help investigate current and model legal, legislative, and administrative policies that bear on the financial security of poultry farmers.

> The Institute has also identified an Agricultural Extension attorney and economist to help with the research phases of the project. In addition, Farmers Legal Action Group (FLAG), national leaders in litigation and investigation of progressive farm policy, are interested in becoming deeply involved in the project. Farm leaders and farm organizations from across the country have also expressed an interest in helping, because they recognize that the poultry contract system is moving into other sectors of agriculture with tremendous consequences for the economic future of the family farmer.

The North Carolina Center for Nonprofits provides a simple, straightforward staffing section, mainly describing the credentials of the project director for the new organization.

> The project director for this 1991 project will be Jane Kendall, who has been in nonprofit leadership for 12 years at the National Society for Internships & Experimental Education (NSIEE). She has worked 18 years to get young people involved in nonprofits, from starting a student community service at the University of North Carolina at Chapel Hill in 1972, to directing southern regional programs to engage young people in community-based economic development and to help environmental groups use interns more effectively, to producing a three-volume resource book in 1990 entitled *Combining Service and Learning*, which is a collaborative project of 93 national nonprofits. A founding Board member of ACCESS: Networking in the Public Interest, she also chairs United Way's Triangle Management Assistance Program, serves as a foundation trustee, and is active in several environmental groups. As a Kellogg Foundation National Fellow, she has met with nonprofit leaders across the country and visited programs in seven states that offer workable models for addressing the needs of North Carolina nonprofits. She will leave her position as Executive Director at NSIEE in November to bring this dream to life.

> The Project Associate and Project Secretary to be hired for this project will be individuals with high energy, deep commitment to the goals of the project based on firsthand experience in nonprofits, strong skills in communications, and familiarity with North Carolina.

Finally, the Center for Responsive Politics presents information about the board as well as key staff.

> An active Board of Directors guides the Center's work. This board is led by two former members of Congress: Senator Dick Clark and Representative Orval Hansen. Until recently, Senator Hugh Scott, a founder of the Center, has also lent his considerable leadership and expertise to the Center. Other members of the Board include individuals with distinguished public service careers: Bethine Church, Peter Fenn, George Denison, Paul Hoff, Steven Hofman, Paul Thomas, Robert A. Weinberger and Executive Director Ellen Miller, as well as philanthropist Peter Kovler, and public relations executive Tim Brosnahan.
>
> The Center's Executive Director—Ellen Miller—has extensive congressional experience, both as a senior staffer in both the House and Senate, and as a veteran of the public interest community in Washington. As Executive Director of the Center for Responsive Politics, she directs and manages all project areas: Money and Politics, Congressional Operations, Congress and the Media, Ethics in Government, and Foundations in Public Policy. In addition, as the Center's Executive Director for the past six years, she has been responsible for providing overall management, program planning, direction and fundraising and outreach for the organization. Ms. Miller is an expert on all aspects of the presidential and congressional campaign finance system, as well as on institutional issues concerning Congress. She has written and spoken extensively on money and politics issues, particularly on the rise of campaign spending over the past decade. She holds an advanced degree in urban and regional planning and has completed extensive studies in public policy research.

> The Center's Senior Research Associate—Larry Makinson—will serve as Project Director for this project. One of the pioneers of computer research on campaign financing, he is the author of four books on the subject, including *Open Secrets: The Dollar Power of PACs in Congress* and *The Price of Admission: An Illustrated Atlas of Campaign Spending in the 1988 Congressional Elections.* As a longtime journalist in Alaska, Makinson won national awards for his reporting both in newspapers and public television. He holds a masters degree in public administration from the Kennedy School of Government at Harvard University.

Describe for the reader your plans for administering the project. This is especially important in a large operation, if more than one agency is collaborating on the project, or if you are using a fiscal agent. It needs to be crystal clear who is responsible for financial management, project outcomes, and reporting.

Evaluation

An evaluation plan should not be considered only after the project is over; it should be built into the project. Including an evaluation plan in your proposal indicates that you take your objectives seriously and want to know how well you have achieved them. Evaluation is also a sound management tool. Like strategic planning, it helps a nonprofit refine and improve its program. An evaluation can often be the best means for others to learn from your experience in conducting the project.

Match the evaluation to the project. If you are asking for funds to buy an additional personal computer, it is not necessary to develop an elaborate plan to assess its impact on your operation. But if you have requested $100,000 to encourage people to have blood tests for Lyme disease, you should have a mechanism to determine whether the project's activities achieved your goals and objectives.

Many projects will have rather obvious evaluation procedures built into them. An art institution working on audience development, a settlement house providing an after-school program to disadvantaged children, or a health clinic offering preventive immunization will not spend a great deal of money and time evaluating their respective projects. The number of people served will be the major indicator of the success of these projects.

Not all funders require a formal evaluation; some want monitoring reports only. In this case, it is up to you to decide whether a formal evaluation is an essential component of the project.

Here is the evaluation section from the North Carolina Center for Nonprofits' 1990 proposal. It uses questions to indicate the criteria for determining the project's success rather than describing a formal evaluation.

IV. Evaluation

There will be several measures of this project's success. Can we articulate what the highest-priority needs are? Can we describe all services already available to address these needs—and the remaining gaps? How many forums and interviews were held? In their evaluations, did participants indicate they felt heard and involved? Did we identify key nonprofit leaders across North Carolina? Are they interested? Is a workable database system in place? Is the strategic vision realistic, creative, based on input directly from the nonprofits themselves, and sustainable? Were plans for the Center abandoned if we found that such an organization is not necessary or feasible?

There are two types of formal evaluation. One measures the product; the other analyzes the process. Either or both might be appropriate to your project. The approach you choose will depend on the nature of the project and its objectives. For either type, you will need to describe the manner in which evaluation information will be collected and how the data will be analyzed. You should present your plan for how the evaluation and its results will be reported and the audiences to which it will be directed. For example, it might be used internally or be shared with the funder, or it might deserve a wider audience. A funder might have an opinion about the scope of this dissemination.

Should in-house staff or outside consultants conduct a formal evaluation? Staff may not have sufficient distance from the project to be objective. An outside person can bring objectivity to the project, but consultants may be costly and require time to learn about your agency and the project. Again, the nature of the project and of the evaluation may well determine the answer to this question. In any case, the evaluation needs to strike a balance between familiarity with the project and objectivity about the product or process.

A sample evaluation section follows. It is taken from a study, "Evaluating Foundation Programs and Projects," commissioned by the Saint Paul Foundation.

EVALUATION PLAN: The ABC Literacy Center (ABC)

The purpose of the evaluation for the ABC Literacy Center is to: 1) assess the extent to which intended outcomes and activities are occurring as planned, 2) determine if program components are contributing to program goals, 3) identify areas where improvement in project activity is needed, and 4) identify corrective actions needed to improve project activities.

Evaluation Questions	Information Needed	Data Collection Methods
Outcome Question: What are the intended outcomes of the ABC project?		
ABC will improve the literacy skills of adults	Amount of change in math, reading, writing, and survival skills	Pre/post standardized achievement tests Learner questionnaire
Activity Question: What are the intended activities that will bring about the outcome stated above?		
Instructors will develop industrial learning plans for each client	Progress on plans	Individual learning plans (ILPs)
Learners with reading skills below the 5th grade level will work with volunteer tutors	Number of hours with a volunteer	Client learner log
All learners at ABC will use computers	Number of hours on the computers	Client learner log Learner questionnaire
Strength/Limitation Question: What are the strengths and limitations of the project?		
Staff questionnaire Volunteer questionnaire	Perceptions of strengths and weaknesses	Learner questionnaire
Concern Question: What concerns arose in the course of the project?		
Changes in the project	Concerns on problems	Minutes from staff meetings Staff questionnaire Volunteer questionnaire

6

Developing the Master Proposal: The Budget

The project description provides the picture of your proposal in words. The budget further refines that picture, but with numbers. A well-crafted budget adds greatly to the proposal reviewer's understanding of your project.

The budget for your proposal may be as simple as a one-page statement of projected expenses. Or your proposal may require a more complex presentation, perhaps including a page on projected support and revenue and notes explaining various items of expense or of revenue.

Expense Budget

As you prepare to assemble the budget, go back through the proposal narrative and make a list of all personnel and nonpersonnel items related to the operation of the project. Be sure that you list not only new costs that will be incurred if the project is funded but also any ongoing expenses for items that will be allocated to the project. Then get the relevant costs from the person in your agency who is responsible for keeping the books. You may need to estimate the proportions of your agency's ongoing expenses that should be charged to the project and any new costs, such as salaries for project personnel not yet hired. Put the costs you have identified next to each item on your list.

It is accepted practice to include as line items in your project budget any costs of the agency that will be specifically devoted to operating the project. Most commonly, these would be the costs of supervision and of occupancy. If the project is large relative to the organization as a whole, these lines items might also include telephone, utilities, office supplies, and similar expenses. For instance, if one of three office phone lines will be devoted to the project, one third of the monthly cost of maintaining phone service could legitimately be listed as a project cost.

In addition, most expense budgets include a line called "overhead," which allows the project to bear a portion of the administrative costs, often called supporting services, of your operation. Such items as the bookkeeper's salary, board meeting expenses, the annual audit, and the cost of operating your personnel department might be included in the overhead figure. These costs are not directly attributable to the project but can be allocated to it based on the notion that the project should bear some of the costs of the host organization.

Most groups use a formula for allocating overhead costs to projects, usually based on the size either of the total project budget or of its salaries, as a percentage either of the total organizational budget or of its total salary line. For example, if the project budget is one-tenth the size of the total budget, it could be expected to bear one-tenth of the administrative overhead costs. Funders may have policies regarding the percentage of overhead that they will allow in a project budget. Some do not allow any overhead at all to be included. If possible, you should find out about their overhead policy before submitting your proposal to a particular foundation, because you may need to explain to that funder how you will cover overhead costs from other sources.

Your list of budget items and the calculations you have done to arrive at a dollar figure for each item should be summarized on worksheets. You should keep these to remind yourself how the numbers were developed. These worksheets can be useful as you continue to develop the proposal and discuss it with funders; they are also a valuable tool for monitoring the project once it is under way and for reporting after completion of the grant.

A portion of a worksheet for a year-long project might look like this:

Item	Description	Cost
Executive director	Supervision	10% of salary = $10,000 25% benefits = $2,500
Project director	Full time	to be 11 months at $35,000 = $32,083; hired in month one 25% benefits = $8,025
Tutors	12 working 10 hours per week for 3 months	12 x 10 x 13 x $4.50 = $7,020
Office space	Requires 25% of current space	25% x $20,000 = $5,000
Overhead	20% of project cost	20% x $64,628 = $12,926

With your worksheets in hand, you are ready to prepare the expense budget. For most projects, costs should be grouped into subcategories, selected to reflect the critical areas of expense. All significant costs should be broken out within the subcategories, but small ones can be combined on one line. You might divide your expense budget into personnel and nonpersonnel costs; your personal subcategories might include salaries, benefits, and consultants. Subcategories under nonpersonnel costs might include travel, equipment, and printing, for example, with dollar figure attached to each line.

Three very different expense budgets follow. Note that all of them give the budget period as part of the heading. In the first, there are no subcategories, but staffing expenses are combined under two categories, project staff and support staff.

Expense budget for project to train workshop leaders in special events fundraising—May 1992 through April 1993	
Project staff coordinator plus one-third time program associate	$40,000
Part-time clerical and administrative support	4,000
FICA and benefits	4,000
Consultants	2,500
Travel (24,000 miles)	4,800
Phone	3,000
Postage	2,500
Supplies, research materials	1,800
Printing, copies	5,000
Rent	5,000
Total	**$72,600**

The next budget is more complex, and subcategories are used to group costs. Note that this budget is for more than one year.

Research project on differences in communication styles between men and women—September 1, 1992 through November 1, 1993	
I. Staff	
Executive director (1/3 time)	$ 25,000
Project director (full-time)	52,500
Research assistant (full-time)	35,000
Executive assistant (half-time)	13,000
Interns	7,500
Health Benefits	3,150
FICA/Social Security	9,162
Subtotal	$145,312

II. General overhead costs	
Rent and utilities	$14,000
Office supplies	1,400
Copy service	3,500
Telephone	3,500
Postage	2,000
Courier	1,200
Accounting services	3,500
Legal counsel	7,000
Miscellaneous	2,000
Subtotal	$38,100
III. Computer costs	
Macintosh IICi with monitor	$12,000
9-track tape reader	4,000
FEC tapes and download costs	5,000
Software	2,500
Subtotal	$23,500
IV. Distribution cost	
Press conference	$1,000
Purchase of promotional copies	5,000
Subtotal	$6,000
Total	**$212,912**

The final example is of interest because the amounts requested from the foundation to which it is being sent are separated from the rest of the budget on a line-by-line basis.

Expense Budget for Nonprofit Training Center— January 1 through December 31, 1993		
	For the proposed grant from the ABC Foundation	For the entire project and organization
Personnel (project director, project associate, project secretary, and 3 interns)	$47,000	$95,000
Consultants	1,000	10,000
Travel	6,000	21,000
Meeting expenses (meals, room rental, breaks, AV)	1,300	1,300
Equipment (computer, typewriter, postage meter, copier, basic furniture)	1,500	12,500
Telephone	1,600	5,000
Supplies	900	3,500
Printing and production (surveys, cover letters, invitations to focus groups and forums, follow-up reports, strategic plan, etc.)	1,500	8,000
Mailing (surveys, invitations, drafts, meeting reports)	1,000	5,000
CPA & legal oversight	800	2,800
Survey design, entry, and analysis	1,000	10,000
Office rent ($650/month plus $300 insurance)	2,000	8,100
Employee benefits (20% of salaries—social security taxes, workmen's compensation, insurance)	9,400	19,000
Totals	$75,000	$201,200

Support and Revenue Statement

For the typical project, no support and revenue statement is necessary. The expense budget represents the amount of grant support required. But if grant support has already been awarded to the project, or if you expect project activities to generate income, a support and revenue statement is the place to provide this information.

In itemizing grant support, make note of any earmarked grants; this will suggest how new grants may be allocated. The total grant support already committed should then be deducted from the "Total Expenses" line on the expense budget to give you the "Amount to be Raised" or the "Balance Requested."

Any earned income anticipated should be estimated on the support and revenue statement. For instance, if you expect fifty people to attend your performance on each of the four nights it is given at $10 a ticket, and if you hope that twenty of them will buy the $5 souvenir book each night, you would show two lines of income, "Ticket Sales" at $2,000 and "Souvenir Book Sales" at $400. As with the expense budget, you should keep backup worksheets for the support and revenue statement to remind yourself of the assumptions you have made.

Because an earned income statement deals with anticipated revenues, rather than grant commitments in hand, the difference between expenses and revenues is usually labeled "Balance Requested," rather than "Amount to be Raised." The funder will appreciate your recognition that the project will earn even a small amount of money—and might well raise questions about this if you do not include it in your budget.

Now that your budget is complete, take the time to analyze it objectively. Be certain that it is neither too lean nor on the high side in the expense estimates. If you estimate too closely, you may not be able to operate within the budget. You will have to go back to funders already supporting the project for additional assistance, seek new donors, or underwrite part of the cost out of general operating funds. None of these alternatives is attractive.

Consistently overestimating costs can lead to other problems. The donor awards a grant expecting that all of the funds will support the project, and most will instruct you to return any funds remaining at the end. If you have a lot of money left over, it will reflect badly on your budgeting ability. This will affect the funder's attitude toward any future budgets you might present.

Finally, be realistic about the size of your project and its budget. You will probably be including a copy of the organization's financial statements in the appendix for your proposal. A red flag will be raised with the proposal reviewer if the budget for a new project rivals the size of the rest of your operation.

If you are inexperienced in developing proposal budgets, you should ask your treasurer or someone who has successfully managed grant funds to review it for you. This can help you spot obvious problems that need to be fixed, and it can prepare you to answer questions that proposal reviewers might raise, even if you decide not to change the budget.

Budget Narrative

A narrative portion of the budget is used to explain any unusual line items in the budget and is not always needed. If costs are straightforward and the numbers tell the story clearly, explanations are redundant.

If you decide a budget narrative is needed, you can structure it in one of two ways. You can create "Notes to the Budget," with footnote-style numbers on the line items in the budget keyed to numbered explanations. If really extensive or more general explanation is required, you can structure the budget narrative as just that—straight text. Remember, though, the basic narrative about the project and your organization belong elsewhere in the proposal, not in the budget narrative.

The finalized budget, whether one page or several, is now ready to include in the proposal document. Keep a copy of it with your backup worksheets in a special folder. The materials in this folder will assist you in tracking actual expenses as the project unfolds. They will enable you to anticipate lines that will go over budget or areas where you might have extra funds to spend, so that you can manage effectively the grant funds that you receive. These materials will also be extremely helpful when it comes time to write the grant report.

7

Developing the Master Proposal: Organization Information and Conclusion

Organizational Information

Normally a resume of your nonprofit organization should come at the end of your proposal. Your natural inclination may be to put this information up front in the document. But it is usually better to sell the need for your project and *then* your agency's ability to carry it out.

It is not necessary to overwhelm the reader with facts about your organization. This information can be conveyed easily by attaching a brochure or other prepared statement. In two pages or less, tell the reader when your nonprofit came into existence;

state its mission, being certain to demonstrate how the subject of the proposal fits within or extends that mission; and describe the organization's structure, programs, and special expertise. Here's an example of a concise but effective organizational statement.

> The Center to Prevent Handgun Violence is a national 501(c)(3)(h) education, legal action and research organization founded by Pete Shields in 1983 to inform the public about the scope of handgun violence and to educate Americans about the risks and responsibilities of handgun ownership. Pete's son was murdered with a handgun—an incident that changed his family's life forever and changes the lives of so many Americans each day. The Center works with influential intermediaries from the education, health, legal, law enforcement and entertainment communities to help develop and deliver public safety messages.

Discuss the size of the board, how board members are recruited, and their level of participation. Give the reader a feel for the makeup of the board. (You should include the full board list in the appendix.) If your agency is composed of volunteers or has an active volunteer group, describe the function that the volunteers fill. Provide details on the staff, including numbers of full- and part-time staff, and their levels of expertise.

Describe the kinds of activities in which your staff engage. Explain briefly the assistance you provide. Describe the audiences you serve, any special or unusual needs they face, and why they rely on your agency. Cite the number of people who are reached through your programs.

Tying all of the information about your nonprofit together, cite your agency's expertise, especially as it relates to the subject of your proposal.

This information, coupled with the attachments you'll supply in the appendix, is all that the reader will require at this stage. Keep in mind that the funder may wish to check with other sources to help evaluate your organization and its expertise.

These sources might include experts in the field, contacts they have at organizations similar to your own, other funders, or even agencies such as the Council of Better Business Bureaus' Philanthropic Advisory Service or the National Charities Information Bureau, which issue reports on some of the larger, national groups.

Here is an example from the proposal of the Center for Responsive Politics. In a brief manner, this excerpt describes the organization and establishes its credentials.

Center Experience

The *Center for Responsive Politics* is uniquely qualified to undertake this project. Our previous work in compiling the original *Open Secrets* was but one example of the type of meticulous, even-handed research that has won the Center the respect of news organizations, researchers, academics, grass-roots activists and observers of the American political system. As the nation's only bipartisan research group specializing exclusively in the study of Congress, the Center has produced more than 16 reports, monographs and books offering new insights into the way Congress—and indeed our government—works in response to the needs and aspirations of the American people.

The study of campaign financing has been a major part of that effort, and the Center has produced studies examining the role of money in the 1984, 1986 and 1988 congressional elections. The Center has also been a leader in researching the role of "soft money" in federal elections. Its most recent study in that area, Soft Money '88, examined soft money contributions in nine key states during the 1988 presidential campaigns.

Other research efforts by the Center have included a study of voter registration organizations active in the 1984 elections and a study of political foundations associated with federal office holders or candidates. In February 1988, the Center completed a project based on interviews with 50 directors of political action committees—*PACs on PACs: The View From the Inside;* and a major survey project on free media use by 1986 congressional candidates, the findings of which were published in *Beyond the 30-Second Spot: Free Media Use by Congressional Candidates*. This study was the first time the Center worked with challengers and incumbents surveying 141 House and 40 Senate candidates—nearly 25 percent of all major party candidates who ran for Congress in 1986. Early in 1990, the Center completed an examination of the relationship of the media, the public and Congress—*Dateline: Capitol Hill*. This study was based on a national opinion poll and in-depth interviews with 100 journalists, editors and news producers who cover Congress.

Conclusion

Every proposal should have a concluding paragraph or two. This is a good place to call attention to the future, after the grant is completed. If appropriate, you should outline some of the follow-up activities that might be undertaken, to begin to prepare your funders for your next request. Alternatively, you should state how the project might carry on without further grant support.

This section is also the place to make a final appeal for your project. Briefly reiterate what your nonprofit wants to do and why it is important. Underscore why your agency needs funding to accomplish it. Don't be afraid at this stage to use a bit of emotion to solidify your case.

Three examples follow. The first is the conclusion to the proposal from the Center to Prevent Handgun Violence. It is a strong restatement of the facts that appeared in the body of the proposal.

Conclusion

More than any other time in history, Americans are concerned about the handgun violence that has turned our streets, homes, and schools into battle zones. The Center works to transform this concern into action that will ultimately reduce handgun violence. These efforts reach every facet of American life where people are informed about important issues—

> from television to the courts to our schools. Over the next year, the Center hopes to reach millions more Americans with our handgun violence prevention message. To achieve this, the Center will continue to test and develop messages for effective school curricula. The Center will attempt to bring greater legal responsibility to the commerce and ownership of handguns. The Center will recruit additional authority figures and intermediaries, including law enforcement officials, educators, pediatricians, family doctors, and influential individuals from the entertainment industry, to reach greater audiences and continue its efforts to alleviate the tragic handgun violence epidemic in this country.

The second is the conclusion to the Christian College Coalition's proposal. It is simple, straightforward, and engages the funder directly.

> The potential is very high for this project to result in significant beneficial outcomes for the Christian College Coalition membership. The strengthened professionalism of presidents, trustees and development officers can only heighten their fund raising effectiveness. Because of the needs that will be met as identified in the planning grant, and because of the resulting outcomes which are consistent with the philosophy and concerns of Lilly Endowment, Inc, we are grateful for your serious consideration of funding this project. It will serve to strengthen these colleges, private higher education and our society in general.

The concluding paragraph from the proposal of the Institute for Southern Studies is also simple, and it is inspirational in content.

While the Institute may not be ideally suited as the long-term host for the poultry growers' network, it is the appropriate sponsor at this point given its commitment to the issue, staff leadership, involvement with other reform efforts in the poultry industry (food safety, worker health, and animal rights), and its relationship with the other participants and farm leaders. The momentum is in our favor; the time for action is now. We have an excellent team of people ready to move this project forward and achieve meaningful results. A portion of the funds have already been raised, and other sources have been identified. We encourage your support to make the project a reality.

The main portion of your proposal document is now complete. You next need to put the whole proposal package together.

8

Packaging the Proposal

Writing a well-articulated proposal represents the bulk of the work in preparing a solid proposal package. The remaining work is to package the document for the particular funder to whom it is being sent, based on your research and your contact with that funder to date (see Chapters 10 and 11).

Be sure to check the foundation's instructions for how and when to apply. Some foundations will accept proposals at any time. Others have specific deadlines. Foundations will also differ in the materials they want a grant applicant to submit. Some will list the specific information they want and the format you should adopt. Others will have an application form. In the course of the interviews for this book, it became apparent that an increasing number of foundations are developing an application form or a specific proposal format as a means to help staff look at diverse information in a concise and consistent manner. Whatever the foundation's guidelines, pay careful attention to them—and follow them.

Andrew Lark, cotrustee of the Frances L. and Edwin L. Cummings Memorial Fund, makes this point: "It's amazing to see how many people get our guidelines and don't follow them."

In the following pages we will discuss the packaging of the document, including:

- cover letter or letter of transmittal.

- cover and title pages.

- table of contents.

- appendix.

The Cover Letter

Often the cover letter is the basis for either consideration or rejection. Donna Dunlop, senior program officer of the DeWitt Wallace-Reader's Digest Fund, states, "It should indicate the scope of the project, how it fits into our guidelines and what the agency wants. This should be stated clearly in the first two paragraphs. Don't swamp us with tons of information about history or the history of the problem. Tell us what you want right away. The request should jump off the page. Don't make us guess."

Hildy Simmons advises, "The key is to make sure you are not locked out early in the process. Realistically, with so many requests, we look for reasons to say 'no' rather than 'yes.' The cover letter is the most important piece of the request. It needs to grab your attention immediately so the assistant knows how to direct your request. The cover letter puts you in the right frame of mind in which to sort it out. Otherwise it will be rejected right away."

What a waste for your agency's resources to invest time, energy, and money developing a proposal around a terrific project and then not have it read! To avoid this happening, be clear. Be succinct. And state immediately why the project fits within the funder's guidelines.

For example, you might state, "Our funding research indicates that the Foundation has a special interest in the needs of children in foster care, which is the focus of this proposal."

If the proposal does not fit the foundation's guidelines, this should be acknowledged immediately in the cover letter. You will then need to provide an explanation for why you are approaching this foundation.

If at all possible, the cover letter should refer to the conversation that you have already had with someone in the funder's office prior to submitting the proposal. For example, you might say, "I appreciate the time Jane Doe of your staff took to speak with me on December 1 about the Foundation." But do *not* imply that a proposal was requested if in fact it was not.

Sometimes in a discussion with a funder you will be told, "I can't encourage you to submit because.... However, if you want, you can go ahead and submit anyway." In this case, you should still refer to the conversation but your letter should demonstrate that you heard what the funder said. Joseph Cruickshank, secretary of the Clark Foundation, encourages people to call, but he wants any subsequent letter to reflect that conversation: "Don't say 'At your suggestion, I am writing....' I haven't encouraged anyone to send in a request in the last ten years. If I've talked to you on the telephone, it is helpful to say, 'Following our discussion, I am sending....'

The cover letter should also indicate what the reader will find in the proposal package. For example: "You will find enclosed two documents for your review. The first is a concise description of our project. The second is an appendix with the documents required by the Foundation for further review of our request."

Cite the name of the project, a precis of what it will accomplish, and the dollar amount of the request. For example: "Our After School Recreational Program will meet the educational and recreational needs of 50 disadvantaged Harlem children. We are seeking a grant of $25,000 from the Foundation to launch this project."

In the concluding paragraph of the cover letter, you should request a meeting with the funder. This can take place at the funder's office or on site at your agency. Also indicate your willingness to answer any questions that might arise or to provide additional information as required by the funder.

In summary, the cover letter should:

- state why you are approaching this funder;

- mention any prior discussion of the proposal;
- describe the contents of the proposal package;
- briefly explain the project;
- indicate the size of the request; and
- offer to set up a meeting and to provide additional information.

Who should sign the letter? Either the chairman of the board or the chief executive officer of your agency should be the spokesperson for all proposal submissions. Some funders insist on signature by the chairman of the board, indicating that the proposal has the support and endorsement of the board. However, signature by the executive director may allow for a sense of continuity that a rotating board chair cannot provide. If your group has no full-time staff, then the issue is resolved for you, and the board chairman should sign all requests. This would hold true also if your agency is in the process of searching for a new chief executive.

The proposal cover letter should never be signed by a member of the development staff. These individuals do the research, develop the proposals, and communicate with the funder, but generally they stay in the background when it comes to the submission of the proposal and any meetings with the funder. The individual who signs the cover letter should be the same person who signs subsequent correspondence, so that the organization has one spokesperson.

Variations may occur under special circumstances. For example, if a board member other than the chairperson is directly soliciting a peer, the cover letter should come from him or her. Alternatives would be for the letter to be signed by the chairman of the board and then for the board member to write a personal note on the original letter, or to send along a separate letter endorsing the proposal.

Following is a cover letter to the Lilly Endowment from the Christian College Coalition. Note that the letter includes:

- the request;
- reference to a prior grant from the Endowment to the Coalition; and
- a promise to supply additional information.

20 September 1990
Mr. Charles A. Johnson
Vice President for Development
Lilly Endowment, Inc.
P.O. Box 88068
Indianapolis, IN 46208

Dear Mr. Johnson:

Enclosed is a request for $510,000 ($170,000 per year for three years) to improve fund raising effectiveness among Christian College Coalition institutions.

The thought and content of this request has resulted from about 18 months of study and discussion which was initiated by the Lilly Endowment, Inc. planning study grant. Even this week, Project Director, Dr. Wesley Willmer, was using the results for workshops at the Christian Stewardship Association national conference in Kansas City, Missouri. The benefits of the planning grant continue to be evident and we look forward with anticipation to the significant outcomes possible as a result of this proposed project.

By early November, and before your board meeting, we expect to have off the press and to you a new edition of the Peterson's Guide prepared in cooperation with the Coalition, *Consider a Christian College*, and the edited monograph from the planning study grant entitled *Friends, Funds and Freshmen: A Manager's Guide to Christian College Advancement*.

If you have further questions or need additional information, please feel free to call on me.

Please accept my sincere gratitude for all you have done to assist in the planning study and in guiding our follow-work with this proposal process.

Cordially,

Myron S. Augsburger

jw
Enclosure

Here is another example of a cover letter, this one from Rena-Coa, a New York City-based youth organization. It has the following characteristics:

- It is very brief.
- It succinctly describes the agency.
- It introduces the project.
- It offers additional information and an opportunity to meet.

Dear _____:

I am writing to introduce you to RENA-COA Multi-Service Center, Inc. and to request the support of _____ for our programs for children and adolescents in Upper West Harlem and Washington Heights.

Since 1969, RENA-COA has responded to the need for positive and responsive programs for young people in our community. Perhaps at no other time in our history, however, has this need been so great. We see it manifested in the growing number of dropouts and jobless youth who stand on street corners with nothing to do and nowhere to go. More alarming is the recent rise in teen pregnancies, drug abuse, and street crimes.

Our answer has been a reinvestment of time, funds and energy to develop and revitalize four core programs for youth. These are: an afterschool and summer tutorial program; a gameroom and arts and crafts center for "latchkey" children; a youth development and recreation program; and a basketball league that combines competition with counseling.

A proposal outlining our programs in detail, as well as supporting documents, are enclosed for your further review. Should you need additional information or would like to meet to discuss our request, please do not hesitate to call me.

Sincerely,

Samuel R. Poinsette
Executive Director

SRP:ca

Enclosures

Cover Page and Title

The cover page has three functions:

1. to convey specific information to the reader;

2. to protect the proposal; and

3. to reflect the professionalism of the preparer.

You should personalize the information on the cover page by including the name of the funder. You might present the information as follows:

A PROPOSAL TO THE XYZ FOUNDATION

or

A REQUEST DEVELOPED FOR THE XYZ FOUNDATION

Then note the title of the project:

A CAMPAIGN FOR STABILITY

Provide key information that the funder might need to contact your agency:

Submitted by:

Mary Smith
Executive Director
The Nonprofit Organization
40 Canal Street
New York, NY 10013
212-935-5300

It is possible that your cover letter will be separated from the rest of the proposal. Without key information on the cover page, the funder could fail to follow up with your agency.

This cover page from the Christian College Coalition proposal to the Lilly Endowment serves as an example.

---

20 September 1990

FOR: Lilly Endowment, Inc.
P.O. Box 88068
Indianapolis, IN 46208
Dr. Charles A. Johnson
Vice President for Development

FROM: Christian College Coalition
329 Eighth St. NE
Washington, D.C. 20002
Dr. Myron S. Augsburger
President

RE: $510,000 request to improve fund raising effectiveness in Christian liberal arts colleges and universities

---

The title you assign to your proposal can have a surprisingly significant impact on the reader. It should reflect what your project is all about. "A CAMPAIGN FOR STABILITY" tells the reader that there is a formal effort taking place and that the result will be to bring stability to the nonprofit applicant. It is short and to the point, while being descriptive.

There are a few suggestions for developing the title for a proposal:

- Don't try to be cute. Fundraising is a serious matter. A cute title implies that the proposal may not be a serious attempt to solve a real problem.

- Try not to duplicate the title of another project in your agency or one of another nonprofit that might be well known to the funder. It can cause confusion.

- Be sure the title means something. If it is just words, try again, or don't use any title at all.

Coming up with the title can be a tricky part of proposal writing. If you are stuck, try these suggestions:

- Seek the advice of the executive director, the project director, or a creative person in the organization or outside.

- Hold an informal competition for staff or volunteers to see who can come up with the best title.

- Go to the board with a few ideas and ask board members to select the one that makes the most sense.

- Jot down a list of key words from the proposal. Add a verb or two and experiment with the word order.

Let's take a look at a few actual titles and evaluate their effectiveness.

Title	Effectiveness
Forward Face	Arouses interest but does not tell you anything about the project.
	This is a proposal that seeks funds for facial reconstruction for disfigured children. With the help of the nonprofit group involved, the children will have a new image with which to face the future. The title is a pun, cute but not very effective.
Vocational, Educational Employment Project	This title tells us that three types of services will be offered
	The project serves disadvantaged youth, which is not mentioned. The effectiveness of this title could be improved if the population served were somehow alluded to.
Building a Healthier Tomorrow	This title implies that construction will occur, and indeed it is the title for a capital campaign. It also suggests that the construction is for some kind of health facility.
	This proposal is for a YMCA to improve its health–wellness facilities. Thus, the title is very effective in conveying the purpose of the proposal.

You should evaluate any titles you come up with by anticipating the reaction of the uninitiated funding representative who will be reading this proposal.

Table of Contents

Simply put, the table of contents tells the reader what information will be found in the proposal. The various sections should be listed in the order in which they appear, with page numbers indicating where in the document they can be located. The table should be laid out in such a way that it takes up one full page.

Following the proposal format we've recommended, a table of contents would look like this:

TABLE OF CONTENTS	Page
Executive Summary	1
Statement of Need	2
Project Description	4
Budget	7
Organization Information	9
Conclusion	10

By stating where to find specific pieces of information, you are being considerate of the proposal reader, who may want an overview of what information is included but may also want to be selective in the initial review.

The Appendix

The appendix is a reference tool for the funder. Include in it any information not included elsewhere that the foundation or corporate grantmaker indicates is required for review of your request. Not every proposal requires one.

The appendix should be stapled together separately from the proposal narrative. Because it usually contains information that the funder has specifically requested, keeping it separate makes it easy for the funder to find. The appendix may have its own table of contents indicating to the reader what follows and where to find it.

A sample table of contents to a proposal appendix follows. It is taken from a proposal from the East Side House Settlement.

Appendix

East Side House Settlement Proposal Table of Contents

I. Board of Managers

II. I.R.S. Letter of Determination

III. Operating Budget

IV. Financial Statement

V. 990 Form

You may wish to include any or all of the following items in the appendix:

1.   A board list. This should contain the name of each board member and that person's business or other affiliation. Adding further contact information such as address and telephone number is optional. The reader will use this to identify people he or she knows or whose names are familiar.

An excerpt from the board list for East Side House Settlement is provided as an example.

2. Your nonprofit's IRS Letter of Determination. This document, issued by the IRS, indicates that your agency has been granted 501(c)(3) status and is "not a private foundation." Gifts made to your organization are deductible for tax purposes. This letter is often requested by funders. Foundations can give most easily to publicly supported organizations, and corporations want their gifts to be tax deductible.

3. Financial information. The operating budget for the current fiscal year, and the latest audited financial statement are often appropriate to include. Some funders request your latest 990 in order to make an assessment about the financial stability of your organization. If your agency is religiously affiliated and you do not file a 990, you will need to explain this fact to a funder that requests it.

4. Resumes of key staff. If the background information on key staff members is not included as part of the project statement of the proposal, it should be included in the appendix. This also might be the place to include the organization chart, if you feel it would be helpful.

Do not include in the appendix anything that is not required by the funder or deemed essential to making your case. The key is to give the funder what is needed for review of your proposal without making the package look overwhelming. For example, many nonprofits like to add press clippings to the appendix. If they make the package appear unnecessarily bulky and are tangential to the grant review, they should be sent to the funder at another time when they will receive more attention. However, should these clippings be essential to the review of the request, then by all means include them.

At this stage of assembling the proposal, you have a cover letter and two additional separately packaged components: the proposal narrative and the appendix. If each is clearly identifiable, you will save the funder time and energy in the initial review of your proposal.

Packaging

Packaging refers to both the physical preparation of the documents and their assembly.

Physical preparation

Every proposal package should be individually prepared for each funder. This permits you to customize the submission in order to reflect the interests of a specific funder and to show them that you've done your homework. This is the point at which you need to double check the guidelines for a funder's specific requirements for the proposal package.

If you are using wordprocessing equipment, it will be relatively easy to customize the cover letter, title page, and other components of the package that have variables in them. For those components that are photocopied, be sure that the originals you are working from are crisp and legible. For example, if your IRS Letter of Determination is in poor condition, write to: Internal Revenue Service, Exempt Organizations Division, P.O. Box 1618, Brooklyn NY 11202, and ask for a fresh copy of the letter. For the other documents, copy from originals whenever possible.

Assembly

When a proposal arrives in a funder's office, any binding is usually removed before the proposal is reviewed. Therefore, do not waste money on binding for the proposal and the appendix. Simply staple each document, or use a plastic strip to hold together each document.

You have three documents: the cover letter, the proposal, and the appendix. The latter two are separately stapled. In all likelihood, these documents will require a manila envelope. Be certain that the addressee and return address information are printed clearly on the envelope. You may want to put a piece of cardboard in the envelope to protect the documents. Then insert the three documents with the cover letter on top, followed by the proposal and the appendix.

With regard to the funder's address, if you are following the procedure recommended in Chapter 11 for submitting this request, you will have had a conversation with the funder's office prior to submitting the proposal. Use that opportunity to verify the address and the name of the person to whom the package is to be addressed.

9

Variations on the Master Proposal Format

In the preceding chapters we presented the recommended format for components of the standard proposal. In reality, however, not every proposal will slavishly adhere to these guidelines. This should not be surprising. Sometimes the scale of the project might suggest a small-scale proposal to match, or the type of request might not require all of the proposal components or the components in the sequence recommended here. The guidelines and policies of individual funders will be your ultimate guide. Some funders state that they prefer a brief letter proposal; others require that you complete an application form. In any case, you will want to use the guide to the basic proposal components (see Chapter 2) to be sure that you have not omitted an element that will support your case.

What follows is a description of a letter proposal and of other format variations.

A Letter Proposal

The scale of the project will often determine whether it requires a letter or the longer proposal format. For example, a request to purchase a $1,000 fax machine for your agency simply does not lend itself to a ten-page narrative. A small contribution to your agency's annual operating budget, particularly if it is a renewal of past support, might also warrant a letter rather than a full-scale proposal.

What are the elements of a letter request? For the most part they should follow the format of a full proposal, except with regard to length. The letter should be no more than three pages. You will need to call upon your writing skills, because it can be very hard to get all of the necessary details into a concise, well-articulated letter.

As to the flow of information, follow these steps while keeping in mind that you are writing a letter to someone. It should not be as formal in style as a longer proposal would be. It may be necessary to change the sequence of the text to achieve the correct tone and the right flow of information.

Ask for the gift: The letter should begin with a reference to your prior contact with the funder, if any. State why you are writing and how much funding is required from the particular foundation.

Here is an excerpt from a letter proposal for the Edenwald-Gun Hill Neighborhood Center:

> Dear _____:
>
> "There Are No Children Here," a recent book by Alex Kotlowitz recounts the story of two young boys growing up in the housing projects of Chicago amid extreme violence, drugs and crime. The boys' mother says that in the projects, there are no children because, "They have seen too much to be children."

For children living in New York City Housing Projects, growing up can be just as difficult. However, at the Edenwald Housing Project, located in the Northeast Bronx, the Edenwald-Gun Hill Neighborhood Center has established a safe haven for youngsters where they are given the opportunity to grow and learn and play. Through the Center's After School Program, children are given the guidance and support needed to overcome the devastating obstacles associated with growing up in the Projects.

The After School Program offers area children a safe, stimulating environment, while providing enrichment activities that augment the school curriculum. The goal of the program is to help children strengthen basic skills and keep up with school work because it recognizes that once a child has fallen behind, school dropout becomes much more likely. It is our hope that the _____ will provide a grant of $____ for this important program.

Describe the need: In a very abbreviated manner, tell the funder why there is a need for this project, piece of equipment, etc.

Here are two paragraphs outlining a need, taken from a letter request for Family and Children's Services located in Elizabeth, New Jersey:

Sweeping social and economic changes during the past two decades have drastically affected the ability of families to function. Dramatic increases in poverty, joblessness, homelessness, AIDS, teen pregnancy, domestic violence and substance abuse contribute to, and are caused by, family and individual breakdown. Pressures from within, and forces from without, threaten the capacity of the family to protect, nurture and guide its individual members. Children in particular are affected, often permanently, by the lack of a safe, supportive and loving home.

According to a recent survey project: "Children in the 90's," conducted by The Janet Memorial Foundation, a significant group of the 123,440 children under the age of 19, plus an unknown number of "aging out" youth, in Union County are at-risk. This is particularly true for children living in impoverished, urban areas such as Elizabethport. Unstable and dysfunctional families are certainly a major contributing factor.

Explain what you will do: Just as you would in a fuller proposal, provide enough detail to pique the funder's interest. Describe precisely what will take place as a result of the grant.

Here's another excerpt from the Edenwald-Gun Hill Neighborhood Center's proposal.

The After School Program

The After School Program serves the children that reside at Edenwald, as well as those in the surrounding community. Through three component programs, the Center helps children stay in school, and teaches them to enjoy learning. A description of the components follows:

Many of the childrens's parents never completed school themselves, and are not able to help their children with homework. Homework Help provides children with individual tutoring in a quiet, comfortable setting. The program has four classes of 35 children each, ranging in age from kindergarten to 6th grade. Each class is supervised by one teacher and several volunteers from a local high school.

Monday through Friday the children are picked up at school in the afternoon by EGH staff and walked to the Center, where they are given a light snack. From 3:30 to 4:30, the children do their homework under the guidance of Edenwald staff. Group and one to one tutoring is provided for children having trouble with assignments. Serious difficulties with school work are reported to the parent(s).

At 4:30 the youngsters have an hour of recreational time where they may participate in organized games or sports. The Center provides dinner to each child at 5:30 through a U.S.D.A. subsidized meal program. The day ends at 6:00, when the parents come to pick up their children.

Provide agency data: Help the funder know a bit more about your organization by including your mission statement, brief description of programs offered, number of people served, and staff, volunteer and board data, if appropriate.

The organizational information from the Family and Children's Services serves as an example.

Family and Children's Services (FACS) has been a lifeline for Union County families since 1893. Founded as the Charity Organization Society, the agency's original mission was to distribute money and coal to the poor. Today, FACS is among the oldest non-profit family and community service organizations in Union County, serving over 2,000 individuals and families yearly.

For 98 years FACS has been committed to strengthening the mental, physical and emotional well-being of the community's children, families and adults. FACS provides a broad range of services including: comprehensive social and psychological services to at-risk youth living in Elizabethport, child abuse prevention counseling, parenting skills training, intensive in-home family therapy, a child abuse prevention program for low-income teenage parents, a therapy program for the homeless and homeless case management, adoption services, and a full range of social and psychological treatment and counseling for all ages and socioeconomic backgrounds.

Include appropriate budget data: Even a letter request may have a budget that is half a page long. Decide if this information should be incorporated into the letter or in a separate attachment. But be sure to indicate the total cost of the project. Discuss future funding only if the absence of this information will raise questions.

Close: As with the longer proposal, a letter request needs a strong concluding statement.

Here is an example from the Edenwald letter.

> Young children, the most vulnerable to negative influences, are also the most receptive to change. The Edenwald-Gun Hill Neighborhood Center helps children to develop self-esteem and gives them confidence in their ability to learn. These children may be the first in their families to succeed at school and not become part of the increasing pool of unemployable adults dependent on public assistance.

Attach any additional information required: The funder may need much of the same information to back up a small request as a large one: a board list, a copy of your IRS determination letter, financial documentation, and brief resumes of key staff. Rather than preparing a separate appendix, you should list the attachments at the end of a letter proposal, following the signature.

It may take as much thinking and data gathering to write a good letter request as it does to write a full proposal (and sometimes even more). Don't assume that because it is only a letter, it isn't a time-consuming and challenging task. Every document you put in front of a funder says something about your agency. Each step you take with a funder should build a relationship for the future.

Other Variations in Format

Just as the scale of the project will dictate whether a letter or a full proposal is used, so the type of request will be the determining factor as to whether all of the components of a full proposal are required.

The following section will explore the information that should appear in the proposal application for five different types of requests: special project, general purpose, capital, endowment, and purchase of equipment.

Special project

The basic proposal format presented in earlier chapters uses the special project proposal as the prototype because this is the type of proposal that you will most often be required to design. As stated previously, funders tend to prefer to make grants for specific projects because such projects are finite and tangible and their results are measurable. Most special project proposals will follow this format, or these basic components will be developed in a letter.

General purpose

A general-purpose proposal requests operating support for your agency. Therefore, it focuses more broadly on your organization, rather than on a specific project. All of the information in the standard proposal should be present, but there will not be a separate component on the organization information. That information will be the main thrust of the entire proposal. Also, your proposal budget will be the budget for the entire organization, so it need not be duplicated in the appendix.

Two components of the general purpose proposal deserve special attention. They are the need statement and program information, which replaces the "project description" component. The need section is especially important. You must make the case for your nonprofit organization itself, and you must do it succinctly. What are the circumstances that led to the creation of your agency? Are those circumstances still urgent today? Use language that involves the reader, but be logical in the presentation of supporting data. For example, a local organization should cite local statistics, not national ones.

Following is an example of a need statement from a general purpose proposal for the Kenmare Alternative High School located in Jersey City, New Jersey.

Kenmare High School is an alternative learning experience for young women who are not able to continue in a traditional school setting. In Gaelic, Kenmare means "nest." The school was established to reflect that definition, to be a nurturing place where students receive skills instruction in a supportive and communal environment. Founded by the Sisters of Saint Joseph of Peace in 1982, Kenmare serves the young women of Hudson County, and especially those in the downtown area of Jersey City. Any woman, regardless of race or creed, aged 16 to 25, who has dropped out of a traditional school setting is eligible for enrollment.

The Women We Serve

The 80 students who currently attend Kenmare mirror the ever increasing female population whose life situations reflect the harsh reality of the feminization of poverty. Sixty-five percent of the student body at Kenmare are mothers with an average or two children per family. Of these families, 53% are female-headed, single parent households. Sixty-three percent of the women receive some form of public assistance, while the remainder are considered working poor. The current student body at Kenmare is 60% Black and 40% Hispanic. The sum total of their experiences reveal stories of deep personal losses, racism, sexism and constant emotional strains. The women that enroll in Kenmare are seeking an alternative to their current lifestyles.

Why Kenmare is Unique

Through a unique and holistic approach to education, Kenmare offers a program that addresses the academic, career and personal needs of these young women. Because Kenmare students usually have responsibilities in addition to school—parenting or support of families—the program is designed to be as flexible as possible while maintaining high instructional standards. For example, students will be excused to take their children to doctors, to attend parent-teacher conferences for their pre-schoolers, or to go to court for child support. The school provides a nurturing environment with individualized programs and small group classes, which never exceed ten students. All staff efforts are designed to meet the needs of students whose success requires intensive staff time and attention.

The program information should describe how your nonprofit organization meets the need(s) just delineated in the statement of need. This section tells the story of what you are doing. Following is the program information section from the Kenmare proposal:

The Curriculum

The Kenmare curriculum is designed as a dynamic process of education which encourages the uniqueness, curiosity and growth of students and staff. The core academic program is fully accredited by the New Jersey State Department of Education and fosters a mastery of specific skills in three major areas: Mathematics, Communication Arts (including Reading), and Social Studies. Other components to the curriculum include a Work Internship/Career Development program, Health and Physical Education, Personal Development and training in typing, computer operations and word processing.

Instruction in each area of the academic program includes basic skills as well as advanced study, depending on the individual needs of students. Each program stresses the relationship between the individual areas of study as well as the day to day experiences outside of school. For example, in Math classes students learn to budget using figures from monthly bills. They are encouraged to join tenant organizations to develop an understanding of the political process. Career Development classes provide contact with the actual world of work.

Communication arts

In the Communication Arts program, students are offered basic reading and writing remediation. Further skill development includes creative writing, public relations, public speaking, journal writing, literature and research. Special courses include *The Program of Excellence*, which is a class designed to help students acquire a thorough understanding of the grammar, syntax and structure of the English language so that they can communicate effectively in the English speaking community.

In addition, Kenmare has implemented a Basic Grammar Course in Spanish to help Hispanic students become more proficient in English by providing them with a better understanding of the structure and grammar of their first language.

Career development/work internship

For the Career Development Program, Kenmare has adopted the Employability Skills Training Series developed by the Life Skills Center at Columbia University Teachers College. The goals of the training series are to enable students to look for, to get and to keep a job. The program is based on wide research and a high level of success with populations similar to the Kenmare student body. Entry into the work field usually involves risk and relinquishment of public financial assistance and health benefits for the young woman; therefore, it is essential that she feel prepared and organized upon entering the working world.

An integral part of the Career Development Program is the Work Internship. This 10 week program provides actual employer supervised work experience in the business/service community. The Work Internship Program has helped many of our students secure meaningful jobs after graduation. Kenmare graduates work in a variety of organizations throughout New Jersey, including day care centers, nursing homes, schools for the handicapped, housing authorities, social service agencies, hospitals and banks. The number of students placed in permanent positions each year also helps to evaluate the effectiveness of the program.

In addition to the Career Development program, the students are offered a wide range of required classes and electives, providing them with a well rounded education.

Health education

Recurring health problems are a common concern to our students. The health courses at Kenmare include *Anatomy, Physiology, Human Sexuality, Pregnancy, Parenting,* and *Infant and Child Care.* Emphasis is placed on nutrition for the individual and family. Special courses on nutrition are taught by instructors from Rutgers University. Students receive certificates from Rutgers for participating in these classes. Also included are courses in *Child Development from Infancy through Adolescence, Personal Grooming, Home Nursing, First Aid and C.P.R. Training, Drugs and Alcohol, Human Relations,* and *Management of Stress.* Medical and nursing personnel from nearby Christ Hospital serve as consultants and part-time instructors.

Capital

A capital proposal requests funds for facility purchase, construction, or renovation, or possibly land purchase or long-term physical plant improvements. Today many institutions include other items in a capital campaign, such as endowment funds, program expansion, and salaries for professors. But, for our purposes, we will discuss the more traditional definition of capital, that is, "bricks and mortar."

All of the components of a proposal will be included in a capital request. Differences in content will mainly be in the need statement, project description, the budget, and the appendix.

The need section in the capital proposal should focus on why the construction or renovation is required. The challenge is to make the programs that will use the facility come alive to the reader. For example, your agency may need to expand its day care program because of the tremendous need in your community among working parents for such support, the long waiting list you have, and the potential educational value to the child.

Your proposal will be less compelling if the focus of the need statement is purely related to space considerations or to meeting code requirements.

Following is a sample section from a capital proposal for the Children's Aid and Adoption Society of New Jersey.

The Need for the Capital Campaign

The cost to purchase, renovate, furnish and relocate to the Program Services Center is $1.3 million. Payments for this capital investment are currently being taken from CAAS's limited cash reserves. Every dollar spent on debt service and renovation means that a dollar is drained from funds to cover non-reimbursed program costs.

Faced with this situation, the Board of Directors authorized a capital campaign to support CAAS's investment, called **Building for the Children.** The importance of this campaign to CAAS and its future cannot be overemphasized. The Board is dedicated to charting the future course of CAAS, with innovative, supportive and effective programs. Swift payment of capital costs will insure that the depth and quality of programs will not be diminished.

The first capital campaign in CAAS's 90-year history, **Building for the Children** is CAAS's first major outreach to the private sector to request charitable financial support. Virtually all of CAAS's annual operating income has traditionally come from restricted government funds and a small number of restricted foundation grants.

CAAS seeks charitable contributions to this campaign from foundations, corporations and individuals. Your contribution can be made as a one-time gift, or as a pledge payable over three years. This support will signify a commitment to CAAS which, in years to come, will give thousands of disadvantaged and at-risk children and their families the ability to handle the overwhelming problems they face in their everyday lives. Your gift to **Building for the Children** is an investment to encourage a healthy life for many of New Jersey's troubled children and their families.

The project description component of a capital proposal includes two elements. The first is the description of how your programs will be enhanced or altered as a result of the physical work. Then should come a description of the physical work itself. The funder is being asked to pay for the latter and should have a complete narrative on the work to be undertaken. You might supplement that description with drawings, if available. These could be external views of the facility, as well as interior sketches showing people using the facility. Floor plans might help as well. These need not be formal renderings by an artist or an architect; a well-drawn diagram will often make the case. Photos showing "before" and drawings indicating what the "after" will be like are also dramatic adjuncts to the capital proposal.

The budget for a capital proposal will be a very detailed delineation of all costs related to the construction, renovation, etc. It should include the following:

- actual brick and mortar expenses. These should be presented in some logical sequence related to the work being undertaken. For example, a renovation project might follow an area-by-area description, or a construction project might be presented chronologically. Don't forget to include such items as construction permits in this section.

- other costs: salaries, fees, and related expenses required to undertake the capital improvements. Be certain to include in your budget the projected costs of architects, lawyers, and public relations and fundraising professionals. Many capital proposal writers fail to adequately anticipate such "soft" costs.

- contingency: Estimates for actual construction costs often change during the fundraising and preconstruction periods. It is therefore a good idea to build a contingency into the budget in case costs exceed the budgeted amounts. A contingency of 10 to 20 percent is the norm; more than that tends to raise a proposal reviewer's eyebrows.

Here is an excerpt from a capital campaign budget of the Reeves-Reed Arboretum in Summit, New Jersey:

Reeves Reed Arboretum Capital Campaign

Capital		$525,000
1. Grounds management/improvement		225,000
driveway embankment landscaping	30,000	
drop-off curb in driveway	10,000	
front terrace leveling/stone wall	35,000	
realignment of floral garden, landscaping and pool	75,000	
boardwalk trail in Red Maple Swamp	26,000	
plant collection, computerized mapping and cataloging, labeling, plant diversification, refurbishing woodland trails	49,000	
2. Restoration of house and apartment		175,000
conform to fire code	12,000	
handicapped accessibility	2,500	
miscellaneous repairs	8,500	
conversion of unusable space to workspace	4,000	
shingle replacement/restoration of main building	145,000	
upgrading carriage house apartment	3,000	
3. Creation of multi-purpose education center		75,000
air conditioning and heating	8,300	
plumbing	5,175	
electrical	3,475	
service	1,875	
carpentry	26,175	
furnishings and educational equipment	30,000	
4. Construction contingency		50,000
Campaign costs		$125,000
Related Planning Fees (Feasibility Study, Long Range Plan)		$ 50,000
TOTAL		**$700,000**

The appendix to a capital proposal may be expanded to include floor plans and renderings if they do not appear within the proposal text. If a video or brochure has been developed in conjunction with the capital campaign, this could be sent along as part of the appendix package.

Endowment

An endowment is used by nonprofits to provide financial stability and to supplement grant and earned income. Often campaigns, designed like capital drives, are mounted to attract endowment dollars. A proposal specifically requesting funding for endowment may resemble either a special project or a general operating application, depending on whether the endowment is for a special purpose, such as scholarships or faculty salaries, or for the organization's general operations. Your focus will be on the following components: need, program, and budget.

The need section of an endowment proposal will highlight why the organization must establish or add to its endowment. Points to raise might include:

- the importance of having available the interest from the endowment's corpus, which will be used as an adjunct to the operating budget;

- the desire to stabilize annual income, which is currently subject to the vagaries of government grants;

- the value of endowing a particular activity of your organization that lacks the capacity to earn income or attract gift support.

The program information section would describe the impact of endowment dollars on the programs of your nonprofit. Provide as many details as possible in explaining the direct consequences of these dollars. Indicate if there might be naming or memorial opportunities as part of the endowment fund.

The budget will round out all of this data by indicating how much you are trying to raise and in what categories. For example, there might be a need to endow 75 scholarships at $10,000 each for a total of $750,000.

Equipment

Frequently, organizations have a need to develop a free-standing proposal for purchase of a piece of equipment, be it MRI equipment for a hospital or a personal computer for an ongoing program. These would require only a letter proposal, but the scale or significance of the purchase may dictate a full proposal. Again, the need, project, and budget sections of the document will be primary.

In the need section, explain why the organization must have this equipment. For example, this hospital has no MRI equipment, and people in the community have to travel great distances when an MRI test is required.

Then in the project section, explain how the equipment will alter the way services are delivered. For example: "The new MRI equipment will serve some 500 people annually. It will assist in diagnoses ranging from structural problems in the foot to tracking the development of a lung tumor. The cost per procedure will be $1,000, but it will save millions in unnecessary surgical procedures."

This budget may be the easiest you will ever have to prepare. Indicate the purchase cost for the equipment, plus transportation and installation charges. Consider whether staff training to utilize the equipment properly and the added expenses of maintenance contracts should be included in your budget with the cost of its purchase.

10

Researching Potential Funders

Once you have drafted your proposal, you are ready to develop your prospect list of foundations and/or corporations that might be interested in funding it. What you learn during this process will help you prepare different proposal packages, as described in Chapter Eight, depending on the specific funder information you uncover.

The foundation and corporate executives interviewed for this book repeatedly advised grantseekers to pay special attention to the research effort. Most felt that sufficient information is available to enable nonprofit organizations to do their homework, thereby obtaining a clear picture of the interests of potential funders.

There are three steps you should follow in your research:

- Compile
- Investigate
- Refine

Compile

Compile a list of foundations, corporations, and other funders whose geographic and/or program interests might lead them to support your agency and the specific projects for which you are seeking funding. Try to be inclusive at this stage. If you think a specific foundation or corporate donor should be on the list, go ahead and include them. Let further research on the source tell you otherwise.

At the compilation stage, you have a variety of resources to draw upon. Check your local newspaper for articles about corporations or businesses in your area. Talk to your local Chamber of Commerce and civic groups such as Rotary and Lions Club. Be resourceful as you compile your list of possible funders.

You will also want to be aware of who is funding other agencies in your community. These foundations and corporations may be likely sources of support for your own agency. This information can be difficult to unearth. Sometimes another local agency's annual report will list their funders; nonprofits occasionally will publicly thank their funders in the local newspaper; arts organizations usually will list their donors in programs. The Foundation Center's *Foundation Grants Index* lists recipients of grants from the top 850 foundations and those that report directly to the Center.

Investigate

Next, take your list and investigate each source. There are definitive resources available to you to research foundations. The IRS requires foundations to file an annual 990-PF form reporting on assets and grants. You will base your research on directories that have been compiled using the 990-PF or from information provided directly to the directory publisher, on materials published by the foundations themselves, or on the 990-PF itself. It is more difficult to obtain information on corporate giving. Corporations may use two grantmaking vehicles: a private foundation and a corporate giving program. If a corporation has a foundation, then a 990-PF will be filed just as with other private foundations. If the corporation has a separate giving program, it is not required to file a publicly available report on gifts made under this program. Some corporations do issue special reports on their philanthropic endeavors, and a number of directories devoted specifically to corporate giving are now available.

Here is what you are looking for in any of the resources you use:

1. A track record of giving in your geographic locale, in your field of interest, or for the type of support you seek, be it basic operating support or funding for construction or equipment.

2. Grants of a size compatible with your agency's needs. (Bear in mind that in all likelihood your project will have more than one funder.)

3. Funders whose resources are not already committed many years into the future and which do not appear simply to fund the same nonprofit groups year in and year out.

Directories

An appendix to this book contains a list of publications you can utilize in your investigation effort. The Foundation Center is the preeminent source of information on foundation and corporate funders. Its own directories and many other directories and resources are made available to the public at its libraries and cooperating collections in sites all around the country. The Center's collections also usually include copies of foundation guidelines, annual reports, and even newspaper clippings on local or national foundations. Where detailed directory or annual report information is lacking, you can examine copies of a foundation's 990-PF on microfiche at one of the Foundation Center's library collections. Call toll-free 1-800-424-9836 to learn of the library collection nearest you.

Directories will most likely be your primary resource in investigating the foundations on your list. But you must not stop there. Often you will find additional or more up-to-date information in other resources.

Guidelines

Many of the larger foundations, as well as community foundations, issue guidelines, sometimes in pamphlet form but often as a section of their annual report. Foundation trustees and staff generally care deeply about the problems in society and struggle to determine the most effective strategies they can use to produce the greatest impact with their funding dollars. When they issue guidelines or announce areas of programmatic interests, these are the result of careful planning and strategy. You should thoroughly review any available guidelines as part of your investigation of a foundation or corporate donor. Some guidelines are very specific, stating goals or even projects to be funded within each area of interest. Others are more general and require further investigation.

If the foundation in question supports only medical research in Kenya, and your agency provides afterschool reading programs for children in Columbus, Ohio, this is not a good prospect and should probably not be on your list. However, if you are doing medical research at Stanford University that has implications for the population in Africa, there is a chance that the foundation might be interested in your work, if not now, then perhaps in the future.

Don't assume that a funder's guidelines from two years ago are still applicable today, particularly when a funder's assets are growing rapidly or it is experiencing a change in leadership. While the foundation probably will not shift its area of interest overnight from the arts to medicine, there may well be subtle changes in emphasis. You need to be aware of these before making your request. Jessica Chao, vice president of the DeWitt Wallace-Reader's Digest Fund, notes, "We get so many proposals where it is clear they are looking at our guidelines from three years ago. They obviously haven't made the effort to learn about our current interests."

The Annual Report

A foundation's annual report may prove to be your most valuable tool in researching a funder. It is important not only for determining current giving patterns but also for projecting future trends. The annual report reflects the personality, style, and interests of the foundation.

In reading an annual report, you should look most closely at two sections. First, read the statement by the chairman, president, or chief executive. Look for clues that reveal the foundation's philosophical objectives. What are the problems in society that the foundation wants to address? What kind of impact do they hope to make with the foundation's funds? This section will also reveal if the foundation is in the process of changing directions. Such a shift presents you with a significant window of opportunity, if your project happens to fit within new areas they want to explore.

The other section to examine is the list of grantees for the past year. This list is the reality test for the stated guidelines. Madeline Lee, executive director of the New York Foundation, goes so far as to advise, "Don't pay as much attention to the rhetoric of the annual report as you do to their grants. These will help you to spot trends before they are articulated."

Check the grants list against what the foundation *says* it wants to fund. You are looking for clues that will illustrate their specific interests. You also want to look for any discrepancies. Do they say, for instance, that they don't fund capital campaigns, yet right there listed under the grants is a donation of $75,000 to the St. Clairesville Community Center to build a new gymnasium? This doesn't necessarily mean that you should keep them on your prospect list for your own gymnasium. It does mean that you should research the foundation further. Many foundations fund projects or agencies with special connections to the foundation or in which their trustees have a particular interest even though they fall outside their stated guidelines.

The 990-PF will not give you as much information about a foundation as its guidelines or annual report will, but if those are lacking, it is the place you can turn to find a foundation's grants list.

Refine

With information in hand about each foundation or corporation on your original list, you should refine your prospect list. Take care at this stage to focus only on those sources that are *most likely* to help your nonprofit now or in the future. Then ask yourself:

- Have I developed a thorough, well-rounded prospect list?

- Is it manageable? Given the need and the time I have to devote to fundraising, is the list too long or too short?

As you winnow your list, one question will arise: Does my project need to fit precisely within a funder's stated guidelines? Guidelines often indicate a particular area of interest, but they should not be viewed as definitive restrictions. A funder may be looking into changing its areas of support precisely at the time your proposal arrives; or someone at the foundation might evince some special interest in your project. Each foundation or corporate funder is unique and responds accordingly. Use your common sense when determining whether it is too much of a stretch to go to the next step in exploring a particular funder.

11

Contacting and Cultivating Potential Funders

Making the Initial Contact

Once you have determined that a foundation is a likely funder, then you must initiate the contact. Some foundations prefer that you call first to see if your project fits their specific guidelines. Be aware, however, that this is not a popular step with all funders. The reality is that the majority of foundations don't have staff to answer the telephones, and those that do are usually over-whelmed with calls and paper work. One funder interviewed for this book adamantly stated, "I hate telephone calls."

If you do decide to call first, be sure you don't appear to be going on a fishing expedition. Funders find this particularly annoying. Your conversation needs to make it clear that you have read their guidelines and want further clarification on whether your particular project would fit. You are *not* making a solicitation by telephone.

Funders caution that, if you do call, listen carefully to what is being said. One funder commented, "It doesn't matter if an organization makes the first approach by letter or telephone call. A telephone call is fine, but frequently the person will interpret the conversation in his or her own way and not listen. They refuse to hear the 'no.'"

There are three objectives to the initial call:

- It promotes name recognition of your group.

- It tests the possible compatibility between the potential funder and your agency;

- It permits you to gather additional information about the funder and about possible reaction to your project *before* you actually submit your proposal.

How should you proceed? First, rehearse what you will say about your organization. You may be given just a few minutes by the foundation or corporate representative. Also, have on hand the background information you have compiled about the potential funder and how much and what you would like them to fund. If there is a prior relationship with your nonprofit group, be aware of the details.

Second, make the call. It would be great if you could speak directly with the president of the foundation or senior vice president in charge of corporate contributions. But this will not often happen. Be satisfied with anyone who can respond to your questions. In the process don't underestimate the importance of support staff. They can be very helpful. They can provide you with key information and ensure that your proposal is processed promptly. Be sure to obtain the name of the person you do speak with so that reference to this conversation can be made when you submit your formal request. This may be your contact person for future calls and letters.

What should you say? Be prepared to:

- Introduce your agency. Give the name, location, purpose, and goals.

- State up front why you are calling. You want to learn more about this funder with the ultimate purpose of obtaining financial support.

- Inquire if you can submit a proposal: Be specific about which one and the hoped-for level of support.

- Request an appointment. Few funders are willing to grant the request for a meeting without at least an initial proposal on the table, but it's always worth checking. As a matter of fact, each time you speak with a funder, you should inquire if a face-to-face conversation would be appropriate.

Variations will emerge in each call, so you must be sharp, alert, and ready to respond to the funder. At the same time, try to seem relaxed and confident as the discussion proceeds. Remember that you are a potential partner for the prospective funder.

Many foundations have no staff or limited office support. Some corporations assign their philanthropic activities to executives with very heavy workloads. The point is, repeated calls may go unanswered. Above all, be persistent. Persistence will set your agency apart from many nonprofits whose leaders initiate fundraising with determination but quickly lose heart. If you cannot get through to a potential funder on the telephone, send a letter of inquiry designed to gain the same information as the call. If your letter goes unanswered, then be prepared to submit a request anyway.

While persistence often pays off, bear in mind what one funder said: "I don't appreciate the aggressive pursuer mode. I just got off the telephone with a development officer from a midwestern college. He said that he and the president were going to be in town and wanted to meet me. I told him there was no point in meeting, since they didn't have a proposal into our foundation. Therefore there was nothing to discuss. He kept insisting, saying that they wanted to come to discuss different projects. I told him that basically it was a waste of everyone's time because then when they did send a proposal, we would need to meet again."

Along the same lines, another said, "It is annoying to meet a board member of an agency at a social event and then get a call saying he'd like to bring by his executive director to meet with me. I always say, 'Send a proposal first.' Otherwise it's a waste of everyone's time. I don't like an organization to go on a fishing expedition."

While these program officers do not like to meet before a proposal is submitted, others say that they would prefer the proposal to be submitted *after* a meeting.

The message here is that, like people, every foundation is different. Foundations, in fact, are made up of people. It is important to listen to, and to respect, what the funding representative is telling you.

Submitting the Proposal

Actually submitting the proposal may seem anticlimatic considering the amount of preparation that has gone into identifying and researching the prospective funders and putting together the various components. But once you have determined that a meeting prior to submission is not possible or is unnecessary, or once you've had the desired meeting, eventually there comes the time to submit the full proposal to the funders on your list.

Checklists may prove useful at this point. You may wish to check and doublecheck one last time to ensure that all requirements of the funder have been met and that all of the pieces of the proposal package are there in the proper sequence. Above all, you will want to be sure that you submit the proposal in accordance with the funder's deadline. If possible, send in your proposal at least two weeks in advance of the deadline. This enables the funder to request additional information if needed.

Grantseekers often wonder whether they should mail in their proposals, send by overnight mail or messenger, or hand deliver them. By far the best choice is the least expensive one. Use regular mail unless there is a very good reason to do otherwise.

Cultivating the Potential Funder

Don't forget to continue to communicate once you have submitted your proposal. Cultivation of the funding prospect can make the critical difference between getting a grant and getting lost in the shuffle.

Knowledge of the funder's situation, and of its procedures for processing proposals, can be extremely helpful in developing your cultivation strategy.

Funders are flooded with proposals. Even if they turn down all that are clearly outside their guidelines, they still get many more than their budgets will allow them to fund. Ilene Mack, senior program officer of the Hearst Foundations, describes the pressure: "Last year we turned down 85 percent of the requests we received. This was up from 80 percent the prior year." Another foundation officer states, "...Three times a day we get a stack of mail that is 18-20 inches high. Many of these requests get immediate denial because they are outside our guidelines."

How can you assure that your that proposal will be one of those to get into the grant pipeline? The ways in which foundations operate differ widely. At some small family foundations, the donor himself or herself will review all the requests. At the larger foundations, program officers receive proposals in specific areas and must take a proposal through a staff review process before a recommendation goes to their board of trustees. Ilene Mack describes her foundations' process: "All requests get reviewed by program staff and a recommendation is made as to their disposition. I am the third person to review a request. Each program officer writes up notes and gives these to me with the proposal."

Many of the larger foundations make a first cut even before the program officers become involved. For instance, Barbara Finberg, executive vice president of Carnegie Corporation of New York, describes their process: "The initial screening is done in the secretary's office. Sixty percent of the proposals are turned down there. It must be clearly evident that the request fits within the guidelines. If it is not within the current guidelines, then there needs to be a clear case for why it should be reviewed for funding."

At the Aaron Diamond Foundation, Vincent McGee sees everything first. He looks at the first three paragraphs of the request to see if it is within the foundation's guidelines. He urges applicants that don't fall within the guidelines to acknowledge this fact right up front. Only then will he look a little further to see if there might be a fit within a specific area where the foundation has an interest.

Charles Johnson, vice president for development of the Lilly Endowment, summarizes the challenge facing nonprofit agencies: "Increasingly, requests for support will outstrip our resources, so we will do less funding of proposals that come in 'over the transom' and more where we have a relationship. Therefore, it is important to cultivate, communicate, and network with program officers. Talk over the telephone, communicate by letter, be persistent, and don't get discouraged if you get turned down."

Several forms of cultivation may be particularly valuable after the proposal is submitted:

- Communication by phone
- Face-to-face meetings
- Using board contacts
- Written updates and progress reports.

Communication by Phone

Normally you should plan to call about two weeks after the proposal package is mailed. The primary purpose of this call is to make sure that the proposal has been received. You have requested a meeting in the cover letter and offered to supply any additional information required to help the funder consider your request. You should therefore ask if it is appropriate to schedule a meeting at the foundation or corporate office or a site visit at your agency. Be sure to ask about the process and timing for the review of your proposal. This will guide you as to when you might call back or send updated information.

Call periodically thereafter to check on the status of your proposal. If you have had no response in the expected time frame, call to find out if there has been a change in the schedule. Ask the same types of questions as you did previously: Is additional information required? When will the proposal be reviewed? Would the foundation or corporate representative like to meet? Be brief. There is a fine line between being helpful and being too pushy.

Each time you call, be prepared to answer the program officer's detailed questions about any aspect of the proposal or of your agency's work. You should also expect to receive calls from your program officer during the course of the proposal review.

Jessica Chao says, "Be sure you are ready when a funder calls to ask questions about your proposal. That phone call may be your only chance to convey the importance of your project and to convince a potential funder of your ability to implement it effectively."

It helps to stay in touch by phone. This gives you a chance to find out what is happening with your proposal and to share information with foundation and corporate givers.

When appropriate, follow up the phone conversation with a note about the next step you plan to take or confirming any new information you provided over the phone. While phone communication is often the most convenient way to keep in touch, you need to be sure that any agreement or information that is critical to a successful outcome of the review process is put in writing.

Face-to-Face Meetings

Appointments can be very hard to obtain. Many funders will not agree to a meeting until the proposal is under active consideration. This might entail assigning it to a program officer, who would then be the person to meet with you. Even when the foundation or corporate representative respects your group or is intensely interested in your project, he or she may believe that a meeting would not be helpful in arriving at a recommendation on your request. However, some foundations insist on a site visit for most or all of the groups to which they make grants.

When you are offered an appointment, you should view this as a very special opportunity. It is one that you must prepare for carefully.

First, be sure that the right team is selected to attend the meeting. If your nonprofit agency has staff, the chief executive officer or executive director should go. The CEO should be able to answer specific questions relating to the project. The other member of the team should be a volunteer, preferably from the board. The presence of the volunteer underscores the fact that the board is aware of and supports the work of the organization. Under the right circumstances, a member of the program staff can be a helpful adjunct, or you must bring along someone who benefits from the good work of your organization. But don't overwhelm the funder by bringing too many additional people to the meeting. Clear with the funding representative precisely how many people plan to attend. If time permits, call a day in advance to confirm the date and remind the funder who is coming. A site visit obviously allows you to introduce the funding representative to a wider range of people involved in your agency or project.

Next, prepare for the meeting. Compile background information about the foundation or corporation. You should be careful to note any prior interaction with the funder, especially if it was less than positive. Develop a profile of the person(s) with whom you are meeting, if this information is available in standard biographical sources or via the grapevine. Your peers in the nonprofit world who are grant recipients might shed some light on the personality and idiosyncrasies of the funder.

Create a role for each of the participants. It is critical that no one sits idle. There should be a dialogue and rapport among the meeting participants.

Last, know precisely what you want to accomplish in the meeting. You won't leave with a check in hand, but you do need to decide in advance what information you want to share and to obtain.

You should expect to accomplish a great deal through the simple process of meeting face to face with the funder. The meeting will establish a personal relationship between the representatives of your organization and of the funding agency. Despite our high-tech world, giving is still a highly personal activity. Hence, the better your rapport with the donor, the more likely it is that financial support will be forthcoming.

Along with getting to know the people at your agency, this will be an opportunity for the funding representative to gain a much better understanding of your group's work. Hearing from knowledgeable people about your mission, programs, and dreams will allow the funder to ask questions, to refine information, and to correct misperceptions.

Equally important, the funder will gain a much better sense of the project for which you are seeking support. Critical information about the proposal, such as the need, methods for addressing it, and the capability of your group to run the program, may be covered during discussion. For this reason, be sure to review the proposal carefully before the meeting.

You must assume responsibility for the agenda of the meeting. Be prepared to:

- Use an icebreaker. The first few times you attend a meeting with a funder, it can be nerve-racking. Break the tension by telling an amusing anecdote, by relaying a true incident of interest to the group, or by commenting about the view or an object in the room where the meeting takes place.

- Introduce all of the meeting participants. This way the funder will know the players and be clear to whom specific questions should be addressed.

- Get down to business. Once introduced, the participants should promptly move on to the real purpose of the meeting: that your group hopes the funder will become a partner with you in getting your project off the ground.

- Remind the funder about the mission and history of your agency. Be thorough but brief in this review.

- Describe the programs you offer. Again, be succinct, but be certain that the funder has a good overview of your services. This is important in case the project submitted for funding proves not to be of interest. The funder may request a proposal relating to a different aspect of your agency's work, having achieved a good grasp of the whole program.

- Describe the project for which you are seeking support. It is critical that you demonstrate the conviction that success is likely. Provide the necessary detail for the funder to understand the problem being addressed and your agency's proposed response to it.

- Keep a dialogue going. It is easy to speak at length about your organization. But it is also easy to bore the funder, and even worse, for you to come away from the meeting not having gained any relevant new information about this grantmaker. Whenever possible, try to elicit the funder's reactions. Inquire about current programs they have funded that address similar problems. Treat the grantmaker as a potential partner. Remember, their dollars have significance only when combined with programs. Listen carefully to their responses, comments, and questions. This dialogue will clue you into the *real* interests and concerns of this potential funder. Don't assume anything.

- Obtain a clear understanding of the next steps. You should determine the following: If anything more is needed for review of the request; when the proposal will come up for review, and how the agency will be notified about the outcome; and, if as a result of this conversation, it is clear that the proposal is unlikely to be funded, what should happen next.

A great deal can be accomplished in a well-crafted meeting, whether at their place or yours. You don't want this process spoiled by extending it for too long. Once it is clear that the objectives have been achieved, you need to summarize the next steps to be taken by both sides and move on to a cordial goodbye. End the meeting while the good "vibes" are still being felt by both sides.

Using Board Contacts

A contact from one of your board members with a peer affiliated with the foundation or corporate funder you are approaching will usually reinforce the relationship you are building.

How do you discover if your board members have contacts that can help with raising funds? First, circulate to all of the members of your board the names of the officers and directors of the foundations and corporations you plan to approach. Ask your board members to respond to you by a certain date about those whom they know. Then work one on one with individual board members, building a strategy for them to utilize their contacts. Another approach is to meet with the board members to talk about individuals with whom they can be helpful. You may find contacts with funders that you had not intended to approach, where having an entree will make a difference.

Knowing that you have board-to-board contact is not enough. You must assist your board member in capitalizing on this relationship on behalf of your nonprofit group. First, develop a scenario with the board member focusing on how to approach the contact. The more personal the approach, the better it is. Second, assist your board member with understanding why this funder would want to help your organization, finding the right language to discuss your agency and your funding needs, and drafting correspondence as needed. Then make sure that the board member makes the promised contact. Periodically remind this individual of the next step to be taken. The groundwork you have done is wasted if the board member never follows through.

Be forewarned that staff of foundations and corporate grant-makers may be concerned about your board members contacting their board members. This is particularly true of professionally staffed foundations where program officers may consider it inappropriate or may view it as interference. Some funders feel strongly that an agency should not use a board contact, even if they have one. Cynthia Mayeda, chair of the Dayton Hudson Foundation, stated, "It will make a board member crazy. Don't even send a copy of a letter. It will not be read. They just send it to me."

Comments from two different foundation officers illustrate other hazards to using board contacts:

> I understand that the assumption is that if you know a board member you have an advantage; however, in our foundation, if a board member knows the agency, he or she is not allowed to participate in the decision-making discussion.

> We encourage an applicant to go to a trustee if they know them, but sometimes it backfires. We have a very democratic process. Often the other board members will shoot down someone who is pushing for a particular project.

At a minimum staff wants to know in advance that a board contact will be used. As one foundation executive noted, "If your board member calls my board member about your proposal being reviewed by us, you can bet I get the next phone call. I would really like to be prepared for it by knowing from you about the planned communication between these guys."

Where you already are in contact with the foundation staff, it is critical to discuss a board contact with them before it is set in motion.

Written Updates and Progress Reports

Written communication helps a foundation or corporate donor learn more about your group and reminds them that you need their support. You should plan to send materials selectively while your proposal is under review. Here are some ideas for what you might send:

- summary reports on what is going on in your organization;
- financial information, such as a new audit;
- newsletters, bulletins, brochures, or other frequently issued information;
- updates/reports on specific projects; and
- newspaper or magazine articles on the project for which you have requested support, the work of your nonprofit, or closely related issues.

It is usually not necessary to customize the materials, but a brief accompanying note always helps to reinforce your relationship with the funder.

12

Life After the Grant — or Rejection

The Initial Follow-up to a Grant

You've just received a grant from a foundation or corporation. Congratulations! What should you do? First of all, you should celebrate. Include everyone within your agency who contributed to this wonderful outcome. Thank them for their help and remind them about what this means for your organization.

Next, send a thank-you letter to your funder. This seems so obvious that one would think it hardly worth stating. Yet nearly 30 percent of the funders interviewed for this book responded to the question, "What is the best thing an organization can do after receiving a grant?" with the simple response: send a thank-you letter.

These are some of the dismaying comments they made: "I find it amazing the number of people that don't send a thank-you note. This is the worst thing an organization can do, especially when our grant letter says 'This comes with the best wishes of (the donor).' Even the simple courtesy of a handwritten note attached to our grant contract letter would mean something."

Julie Rogers, president of the Eugene and Agnes E. Meyer Foundation, reinforces this sentiment and elaborates further: "The worst thing an organization can do is to not send a thank-you letter. Sending a form thank-you that is obviously written by the development officer is not much better. If you've had a good experience with a program officer who has made a case for you to our Board of Directors, then acknowledge that person's help. It's important to remember that it's not one institution giving to another institution. It's about program staff getting to know and better understand program staff at an agency."

The foundation staff are expressing a concern that needs to be taken to heart. Appreciate the investment that has just been made in your agency. Recognize that it is not an institution which is supporting you but the people within the institution. Remember that the grants decision makers feel good about the decision to invest in your organization. They may even have had to fight for you in the face of opposition by other staff and board members. Show your thanks and appreciation for this vote of confidence.

Terry Saario identifies two competing underlying attitudes that can govern the way an agency responds to receiving a grant: "The best thing an agency can do is to appreciate that there is a partnership. The worst thing they can do is to take the money and run."

Remember the watchword of all fundraising—communication. A telephone call to say "Thank you," an update on recent activities, or an announcement of a great new gift are all ways to keep in touch after the grant is made.

Grant Reporting

If a foundation has specific reporting requirements, you will be told what they are. Usually reporting requirements are included in the grant letter; sometimes you are asked to sign and return a copy of the grant letter or of a separate grant contract. Charles Johnson states, "The person responsible for carrying out the project should see the grant agreement so he or she knows the responsibilities. This is a signed agreement, and we want to be sure it is seen by the person responsible."

When a foundation provides formal reporting guidelines, in most cases there will be dates when the reports are due. If they have given you specific dates for reporting, develop a tickler system to keep track of them. If you can tell now that you'll have a problem meeting these deadlines (such as your auditors are scheduled for March and the audited financial report is due in February), discuss this with the funder immediately. If the foundation staff has not heard from the grantee within a reasonable time period after the reports are due, they will call or send the grant recipient a note to follow up. Andrew Lark commented, "It's amazing how many organizations don't follow up even when we outline specific guidelines." If you are going to be late with a report, *let the funder know.*

Some funders want reports at quarterly or six-month intervals, but most request an annual report and/or a final report, two to three months after the conclusion of the project. Even for grants of fairly short duration, foundations often express the desire to receive an interim report. Unless otherwise stated, an interim report can be informal. "We don't expect an organization to spend three days creating an elegant report—just ten minutes to let us know what is going on," states Joseph Cruickshank.

Most funders want a grantee to keep them apprised of important activities and changes. Hildy Simmons says, "Send us newspaper clippings; invite us to something; keep us informed." If you have printed monthly newsletters that you send to funders, Julie Rogers advises, "Put a personal, *handwritten* note in the corner. It will make us more likely to read them. The more personalized it is the better—anything that will make it stand out from the volume of material we receive." Barbara Finberg of Carnegie Corporation counsels grant recipients to, "...consider us an interested party. Send us annual reports, bring milestones to our attention. Invite us to important meetings."

Donna Dunlop says that while her foundation requires a report, an agency "...should do the report for themselves, not us. It is in their best interest to evaluate their project and learn from the process."

The W.K. Kellogg Foundation issues very specific reporting instructions. Their most recent *Final Report Guidelines* provides a useful framework to guide agency staff in drafting a report to *any* funder. While these guidelines are designed for the Kellogg Foundation's grantees, as reflected in the references to the commitment letter, outcomes, questions, and implementation questions, they provide a reliable model for reports to other foundations that may not be as specific in their requirements.

The following guidelines are reprinted in their totality with permission from the W.K. Kellogg Foundation:

Final Report Guidelines

The final report from your project to the Kellogg Foundation is an important document. It is a permanent record of what you have achieved and what you have learned in the process. This report helps to shape future grant-making directions for the Foundation.

The final report has two parts. First, it should address the results of the just-completed project year in terms of what was planned, what was accomplished, and what factors helped or hindered the attainment of goals. Second, it represents a thoughtful, critical synthesis of the important lessons learned and outcomes over the life of the project. (See "Project Director's Opinion.")

The format below may help you prepare a final report by providing a checklist for the critical thinking process. You should be especially attentive to addressing, within this format, the important evaluation questions for your project.

Project Summary

This introduction to the full report tells the reader what to expect by "setting the scene." Succinctly restate the project's intended goals, the strategies you have undertaken to achieve them, and the methods by which you are evaluating these efforts. Weave into this brief summary the important questions for evaluation which were stated in your commitment letter. Note if changes have been made in any goals or strategies.

Progress Toward Goals

A. Outcomes

Respond to the specific outcomes questions for your project. In addition, if not already addressed, please consider the following:

1. Summarize your achievements.
2. Does your experience suggest that original expectations for achieving these outcomes were realistic?
3. Have there been any unanticipated outcomes? What are they?

B. Implementation (processes and day-to-day activities)

Respond to the specific implementation questions for your project. In addition, if not already addressed, please consider the following:

1. Describe activities directed at each of the outcomes listed above and lessons you have learned during the life of your project.
2. If some intended activities were not undertaken, please note them and explain why they were not pursued.
3. What problems arose and how were they addressed?
4. Describe any new activities or modifications and why they were added.
5. Share other pertinent observations/ accomplishments.

C. Context (characteristics of the setting, needs of targeted groups, and external and internal project conditions that may help or impede project success)

Respond to the specific outcomes for your project. In addition, if not already addressed, please consider the following:

1. Describe factors or circumstances (positive and/or negative) within your environment that affected progress toward achieving your goals.
2. How did relationships with other organizations, institutions, or agencies help or hinder your progress toward addressing needs?

Future Plans

A. Has this project become self sustaining? What activities are being conducted?
B. What structure has been established for the continuation of this project?
C. What indications are there that this project can (or cannot) be adopted elsewhere?

Dissemination (½ page)

A. What information from your project has been made available to the field and how?

B. What plans do you have, if any, at this time for disseminating information about your project.

Project Director's Opinion

A. What do you think are the most important outcomes and "lessons learned" from this project?

B. What are the most important lessons that you have learned from this experience?

C. What recommendations would you make to other project directors working in this area or to the Foundation?

Other

Attach to the final report any appendices which will help to clarify information contained in the body of the report. Be selective! Do not include copies of every newspaper article, brochure, or detailed statistics report having to do with the project. If possible, attach a copy of the organizational chart both for the project and for its place within the greater institutional structure. Attach evaluation reports generated during the project if not contained within this report, or submitted with earlier annual progress reports.

The Kellogg Foundation guidelines are particularly applicable if you have received special project support. But don't be concerned if your project does not lend itself to many of these questions. For instance, if you have received $15,000 to hire a tutor for your after-school program, many of these sections, such as "Dissemination," are probably not applicable. Yet others, like "Future Plans," should be addressed in some fashion in almost any report.

Even if you have received unrestricted, general-purpose support, funders want to know what overall goals you set for your agency for the year. Did you achieve them? What were some particular triumphs? What were some particular problems you faced, and how did you overcome them? Or, are you still dealing with the challenges? (Remember, realism is what counts, along with a sense of confidence that you are appropriately managing the grant.) In contrast to the very specific guidelines from the Kellogg Foundation, the New York Community Trust has these very simple reporting instructions:

A condition of this grant is that you submit to us an interim and a final report. The interim report should be submitted by [six months after date of grant] and a final report by [one year after date of grant]. These reports should contain a fiscal accounting of grant expenditures and a narrative describing the following: (a) the objectives of the project supported by the grant, (b) activities carried out to meet each objective, (c) results accomplished and (d) any problems encountered and how they were resolved. They should also include a detailed discussion of activities carried out to secure funding to continue this project once our grant expires.

Remember, these are presented as general models only. If a foundation supplies its own guidelines, then adhere to those instructions.

Seeking a Renewal

In certain cases, you will want to request that the grant be renewed or that a follow-up project be supported. Some funders refuse to give renewed support because they do not want to encourage dependency or because they see their funding as providing "seed money." For example, Charles Johnson says that the Lilly Endowment "...does not generally get a lot of renewal requests. If an agency needs to have renewed support, then a strong case needs to be made for continuing funds."

Other funders require a certain period of time to elapse between the one grant and the renewal request. For instance, the Hearst Foundations currently require three years between grants, and the ARCO Foundation wants an agency to wait eleven months after receiving a grant before requesting renewed support. "Then we want to know how the grant made a difference, what has been accomplished, [and] what continued support will enable you to do," states Eugene Wilson.

If you know that you will want to request renewed support, you should communicate this early on to the foundation in order to determine the best time to submit another request. One funder expressed sincere regret that a project they had funded was doing well and needed additional support but that the agency waited too long before requesting a renewal. By the time the funder received the request, all the foundation's funds were committed for the following year.

Even grants that could be candidates for renewal may be labeled a one-time gift. Ordinarily the phrase "one-time gift" means that the funder is making no commitment to future funding. It does not necessarily mean that no possibility for future support exists.

You should also determine early on the format required by the funder for submitting a renewal request. Some foundations require a full proposal; others want just a letter. This is another illustration of the differences among funders. It reinforces the need to communicate with the grantmaker to determine their particular requirements.

A report on funds expended and results of the first grant is a particularly critical document if you are going to ask for renewed support. However, many funders want your request for renewal to be separate from the report. As Julie Rogers indicates, "It is best to close out one request with a clear document that is just a program report and not a request for funds. It's cleaner to then start with a new grant request." In larger foundations, the report and the request for renewal might be handled by different staff members; therefore, if you submit only one document, your request might not find its way into the proposal system.

Vincent McGee recognizes that "...the renewal request often needs to come before the final report because of fiscal cycles. This is okay. Just be sure not to send the report with a tag line, 'by the way, we need $25,000 more.' It should state, clearly, why you are asking for continued support and be thorough in outlining why you need it."

Following Up on a Declination

The most important response to a rejection letter is not to take it personally. An old fundraising adage is that "Campaigns fail because people don't ask, not because they get rejected." If your proposal gets rejected, it means you are out there asking. You are doing what you should be doing. Hopefully, you have sent your proposal to a number of other appropriate funders and have not "put all your eggs in one basket." A rule of thumb is that you should approach three funders for every gift, or grant, you need. Thus, even if one or two prospects turn your proposal down, you still have a shot at the third.

Some funders will talk with you about why the proposal was rejected, particularly if you had a meeting with the program staff at the granting institution prior to or at the time of submission. A phone call following a rejection letter can help you clarify the next step. Your request may have been of great interest to the foundation but was turned down in that funding cycle because the board had already committed all their funds to projects in the same subject or geographical area. For example, if your request was for an AIDS program in South Chicago, the foundation may have already overspent in that geographic area. A call to a foundation staff member might result in encouragement to reapply for a later funding cycle.

All funding representatives emphasize, however, the need to be courteous in the process of calling once you have received a rejection letter. It is never easy to say "no," and a program officer who fought hard for your proposal may feel almost as disappointed as you are that it was turned down. While foundation staff usually want to be helpful, it is important to recognize that it can often be difficult to tell someone why a proposal has been rejected. And, as one grantmaker stated, "It is even harder if we don't feel the leadership is up to carrying out the project."

One foundation representative described the conflict this way: "I will respect an organization if they call and ask why their proposal was rejected. I will be annoyed, and they may not get a satisfactory answer, but I know that this is what they should do." Julie Rogers encourages organizations to call and "...get feedback. You can ask what you could have done differently, what would have changed our decision. But remember that program officers are swamped and you may get a less than satisfactory answer. So push delicately."

Many funders caution that if you do call, don't argue with them about their reasons or get belligerent. As Joseph Cruickshank advises, "The best thing to do is work with us....Take the cue if the funder is not interested."

Others discourage follow-up calls. Norman Brown, president of W. K. Kellogg Foundation, says, "Our letters always state why the project was rejected. If we misunderstood, then the agency should follow up. Otherwise our decision is clear cut, and we don't encourage an organization to follow up." Barbara Finberg concurs. "It's okay to come back to us if we suggest it. We take people seriously and show respect for what they do. We expect the same. Our rejection letters mean what they say."

One of the worst attitudes to display at any time during the funding relationship is arrogance. This is especially true following a rejected proposal. Here are excerpts of a letter one funder received after rejecting a proposal that was clearly outside the foundation's guidelines:

...have received your letter declining to support our [proposal]. We have viewed your letter and we have taken notice of your very elaborate way of saying, sorry, we can't support your project. However, we find it hard to accept your decision due to the fact that [the Foundation] has supported projects in the past that weren't nearly as important to our social life here in America....We...are hoping that you'll reconsider our proposal for funding....

Needless to say, the foundation did not reconsider funding the proposal.

This is where it is important to take your cue from the funder, either from the rejection letter or from the follow-up call to staff. If you are not encouraged to resubmit, then you probably shouldn't. And don't try to submit it to a different program officer. Terry Saario recalls agencies who have "...tried to resubmit to a different staff member to get around the system." She continues, "We are very focused in our grant decisions, so if a proposal was rejected, then it was for a good reason."

There are times when a funder will encourage you to resubmit the same request at a particular time in the future. If you have been given this advice, then follow it. In your cover letter, be sure to refer to your conversation with the funding representative, remembering to restate, but not overstate, the earlier conversation.

Even if a foundation is not interested in funding the particular project you submitted, by keeping the lines of communication open and remaining respectful you will be nurturing the opportunity for future funding. Should all this sound too discouraging, take solace from the advice of William Bondurant, executive director of the Mary Reynolds Babcock Foundation: "We welcome agencies coming back. One organization was turned down nine times, and we finally gave them a grant!"

Summary Tips

What to do if you receive a grant:

- Send a personalized thank you.
- Keep the funder informed of your progress.
- Follow the funder's reporting requirements.

What to do if your request is turned down:

- Don't take it personally.
- Be sure you understand why.
- Find out if you can resubmit at a later date.

APPENDIX A

What the Funders Have to Say

When foundation and corporate funding representatives were interviewed, they were asked to respond to a variety of questions concerning proposals, grantor-grantee relationships, and general trends in the philanthropic community.

The goal in presenting attributed quotes is not to instruct you on how to approach a specific foundation, but rather to give you an overall sense of shared views while at the same time pointing up the diversity of opinions on many issues related to grantmaking. While a remarkable number of shared opinions emerge from the questions and answers that follow, ultimately, you should strive to understand the individual character of the foundation or other funder you are approaching. It will be clear from these quotations that as a grantseeker, you are approaching people, not faceless institutions. The more you can personalize your approach, the more productive communication will become.

Following are specific questions asked of the funders surveyed and some of their responses.

What are the characteristics of a successful proposal?

A good proposal helps us see how our investment in you will have a long-term impact. It indicates to us your plans for future support. It says the board is committed to this project. (Andrew Lark)

In a good proposal everything is up front and obvious. I have a healthy dose of skepticism [and a] good proposal leaves me with few lingering questions. (Peter Calder)

A proposal doesn't succeed. It's the project that succeeds. A good communication process is important, including calls, writing, and follow up. (Joseph Cruickshank)

We want to see that an agency has clearly thought through its role and policy in the context in which they are operating. The proposal must be clear about the problem and have clear objectives for addressing it. It shouldn't be grandiose. We need to be assured that the organization has demonstrated its ability to do good solid work. It's not good enough to say we need money because we are facing tough financial times. Everyone else is in that same situation. (Joyce Bove)

A successful proposal projects the personality and character of an organization. It clearly articulates the essence of an organization. It also clearly communicates that the organization deeply understands the context in which it is operating. Even bad proposals may try to do this, but it is usually broad hyperbole; for instance, "We are bigger and better than any other organization like us." The reverse is a proposal that is so generic that if you put your hand over the title, you could attribute it to many different organizations. (Cynthia Mayeda)

It's important that the project not sound like it is happening in a vacuum. There should be recognition that others are addressing the same issue and a description of how your project fits into the overall context of the problem. (Donna Dunlop)

A proposal succeeds because there is a congruence of their ideas and our priorities. We are looking for unusual ways to solve problems. (Norman Brown)

The proposal should be a microcosm of the project. We are looking for a good project within our guidelines. We are not only looking for vision, but also the leadership to implement it. We are investing in leaders. (Jessica Chao)

We look for a promising person working in a promising area, evidence that the principal person is remarkable, able, committed, persevering and effective. We foundations win or lose based on our ability to pick these people. We are then assured that the money will be well spent. We also want to be assured that the project is well thought out. We will check references from our resources and contacts. (William Bondurant)

We support talented, entrepreneurial leaders. We want to be able to assess the quality of leadership. (Julie Rogers)

What else do you look for in a proposal in addition to the standard sections?

I like to think of the proposal as a novel. It should be a conversation between the staff of a nonprofit agency and the staff of a foundation. The background information should set the stage. It should give you a flavor of the organization. Anything extraneous, which is not part of the dialogue, should be put in the appendix. (Madeline Lee)

We look for who else has been approached for funds and for what amount. (Andrew Lark)

We want to see a list of other funders and how much they gave. (Ilene Mack)

We are interested in knowing about funders and any others investing in the project. What is the board support? What is the community support? (Jessica Chao)

We want to see a list of the board members *with* affiliations. (Ilene Mack)

We prefer to see a one- to three-page concept paper first, before a full-blown proposal. What we are looking for is the germ of an idea. If it is of interest, we will then ask for the full proposal and a meeting. However, if the full proposal is sent first, this is not a negative. (Norman Brown)

Standard "to whom it may concern" letters included in a proposal are not effective. On the other hand, independent letters sent by others in support of a project can be effective. They are a valid verification of the project and people involved. (Hildy Simmons)

Thoughtful letters of support—not "to whom it may concern" letters—can be helpful, particularly if it's from someone I know and respect. (Julie Rogers)

We are interested in specific outcomes, timetable, other resources, and how information will be disseminated to others. We also need to see that the organization has a demonstrated knowledge of the field. What are other organizations doing and how does their work fit into the puzzle? (Terry Saario)

On what section of the proposal do you put the most weight?

The first three paragraphs of the cover letter are most important. This section should say who they are and what funding they are looking for. I will then look at who the other funders are. I will often call these funders to see how they felt about the organization. Did the organization fulfill the grant request? (Vincent McGee)

The first paragraph is the most important. We want the first sentence to say what the organization wants: "I am writing to request a grant of $10,000 to support an after-school reading program for children of migrant workers in Homestead, Florida." It must be clear from this first paragraph that the proposal falls within our guidelines. If it doesn't, then it must say something like, "I recognize this project does not fall within your geographic guidelines. However, because of your interest in children of migrant workers, I thought you might be interested." It should convince us that we should read further. Within the proposal, the statement of need and the objectives are most important. (Joseph Cruickshank)

The executive summary or one-page summary sheet is most important. This is the first thing we read. I start with the proposal summary and read to the point where I know if it's outside our guidelines. Within the summary, the need is very important. How does the agency diagnose the need, and how is it going to go about meeting it? Then we look at the budget and the projected sources of continued funding. We also look at the board of directors. Does the board reflect the community? Sometimes we will fund a request that comes out of the blue and is not within our guidelines. But in this case it must be something particularly compelling: The problem and proposed resolution hit a chord. (William Bondurant)

We read whatever it takes to determine if it is within our guidelines. Then, even if it fits within our guidelines, it may get rejected because it falls into a program area where we have already committed funds for the year. We like to see that an organization has the people to carry out their proposed project. We look at how the project relates to the mission of the organization. The less it relates, the more likely it is that the organization will not have the staff to carry it out and will have to scurry to find people for this project. (Charles Johnson)

I read the executive summary and the budget first. It is important that any points raised in the summary be amplified in the proposal. I will often look to the proposal for further clarification of a particular point, and I won't find any more information. We want to see what you want to do and why. We look at your mission. We want to have a sense of your capacity to carry out the project. We look at the diversity of your board. Do they represent your community? We also look carefully at the financial statements. (Hildy Simmons)

We first look at the budget. What we are trying to measure is cost per client served, the cost efficiency of the program. (Andrew Lark)

The initial letter of inquiry will indicate the idea and how it fits into our guidelines. The document that goes to the board for their approval is not the proposal, but a document created by the staff. (Terry Saario)

The executive summary or cover letter is most important. I don't want to search for the information on who, what, where, when, and why. If you can't tell me in one page, you can't tell me in ten. (Ilene Mack)

The statement of the problem and how it will be addressed is most important. What is the problem? What is the plan for addressing it? What are the projected results? (Norman Brown)

The executive summary is the most important. This is what gets mailed to our senior management for review and decisions. An organization needs to be able to put in a kernel what they plan to do and the projected outcomes. In other words, what is the problem and how are you going to solve it? (Eugene Wilson)

We have just started sending applicants a one-page cover sheet which should be attached to every proposal. What is most important is a clear articulation of the problem and how the organization is going to tackle this problem with the proposed project. The organization's leaders must demonstrate a knowledge of similar and related projects. Hardly anyone is unique. We look at staff capacity and check references. We will call other funders, government agencies or experts in their field. (Joyce Bove)

What should the cover letter include?

The cover letter is what is shown to our board. It should have a short summary of the project and indicate the geographic area. It should be one or two pages long. (Andrew Lark)

The cover letter should be reader-friendly. It should not repeat everything in the proposal. Take out any repetition. (Charles Johnson)

The cover letter should be succinct. A one page description: here's the project; here's the cost; here's what we are going to do. (Joseph Cruickshank)

The cover letter sets the stage. It should give the vital information relevant to the project. (Terry Saario)

What are you looking for in a budget?

I like to see three years' comparison, last year, this year, and next. But I don't want to see every line item. Don't tell me your stamp budget unless you think it is important for me to know. If there is something that seems unusual, or out of line with other years, then use a footnote to explain. But don't use footnotes to tell me how you arrived at your transportation budget, for instance, 12 bus trips at $5.75 per trip. (Cynthia Mayeda)

We want to know what portion of the budget you are asking us to fund. We also want to know how you will run the program if you don't get all of your funding. (Andrew Lark)

Our financial people review the budgets carefully. Sometimes we will find that as people develop and change a proposal, they forget to change the budget, so it is not consistent with the request. (Charles Johnson)

We like to see the salaries of the principal people and the amount of time they will spend on the project. We want to see the non-personnel expenses spelled out. And we want to know where the rest of the money is coming from. We want to be assured the agency can continue the project. (Barbara Finberg)

We like to see more, rather than less, information in the budget. We want to see how our money will be used, how it will fit into the whole picture. (Ilene Mack)

We like to see the project budget in the context of the larger institutional budget. We like budget footnotes. We also like to see in-kind service indicated, as long as it is something legitimate. (Donna Dunlop)

I don't like to see in-kind service in the budget, because often it is just a million volunteers licking stamps. It can be a bogus attempt to make a $300,000 budget look like a million dollars. (Jessica Chao)

Financial honesty is important. The worst are the computer-generated budgets with little dots and lots of details. These budgets are for internal organizational use and should not be sent to funders. We don't want to see how every $10 is spent. We want to see where your other support is coming from, whether it's government, general support, fundraising, etc. (Hildy Simmons)

A budget should be stated fairly and honestly. Don't overstate your budget. We ask for an income and expense statement at the end of the year and compare it to the original budget. It is important that there be no major unexplained discrepancies. (Peter Calder)

Should the request ask for a specific dollar amount from the foundation?

We will not consider the proposal if a specific amount is not requested. (Andrew Lark)

We want to see the dollar amount and over what period of time it is needed. (Charles Johnson)

The organization should ask for an amount. It indicates they have done their homework. But we don't always pay attention to it. We will sometimes give more and sometimes less. (Joseph Cruickshank)

I don't care if an amount is specified. Sometimes we will give more, and sometimes less, than the amount asked for. (Cynthia Mayeda)

We don't require that they ask for a specific amount in the proposal. (Norman Brown)

How long should a proposal be?

It should be not under three pages or over ten. Seven to eight pages is best. (Andrew Lark)

For us it should be five pages, plus our application form which includes a summary page and financial information. (William Bondurant)

Only write what it takes. The length of the proposal does not relate to the size of the grant. (Charles Johnson)

We don't pay by the pound. A huge telephone book-like proposal gets read last. (Cynthia Mayeda)

We like to see a one- to three-page preproposal first. (Norman Brown)

One to two pages are necessary. An organization needs to put in [the essence of] what it is proposing. If we get a lot of information, it delays consideration. We are so swamped that it goes to the bottom of the pile. (Eugene Wilson)

Two to three pages with backup material in the appendix are fine. But too much back-up is not helpful. For instance, we sometimes get a lot of detailed medical information that none of us can understand—or 30 pages of resumes. This is not of great value. (Ilene Mack)

Our guidelines say two to three pages, but most people have trouble stating their case that succinctly. What is important is to get immediately to the point. (Peter Calder)

Fifteen pages should be the maximum. We are getting more and more good three- to four-page proposals and fewer of the 20-page proposals with huge appendices. That is what we prefer. (Donna Dunlop)

Ten pages. (Joyce Bove, Julie Rogers)

Five to six pages with short, declarative sentences [are sufficient]. (Hildy Simmons)

Three to five pages plus a budget and appendices. (Vincent McGee)

Short. An organization once sent me a 33-page proposal. I read every word and at the end I didn't have a clue what they were talking about. (Joseph Cruickshank)

Three to ten pages. If it's less than ten pages, and it's clearly within our guidelines, then the proposal gets read from beginning to end by three people here. Put anything else in the appendix. Better still, save the trees and don't send the appendix. (Madeline Lee)

If we need more information, we'll ask for it. (Donna Dunlop, Hildy Simmons, Madeline Lee)

Do you like to see newspaper clippings, brochures, videos, anecdotes, and/or statistics?

NEWSPAPER CLIPPINGS

One or two well-chosen articles are good. I get concerned about copying costs if I am sent tons of articles. (Cynthia Mayeda)

Newspaper articles are a waste of time, unless specifically relevant. Then highlight the areas of interest to save us time. (Andrew Lark)

We have limited file space, so I discard most newspaper clippings unless they are particularly relevant to the specific project for which funds are requested. (Peter Calder)

Newspaper clippings can be useful if they reinforce the agency and the proposal. But don't send a whole packet. Just one or two of the most germane. (Eugene Wilson)

If there is a particularly good article describing the organization, that can be good. But I don't like to receive 3,000 articles. I throw most of them away because we just don't have filing space. (Ilene Mack)

Sometimes journalists do a better and more succinct job of summarizing the program because they are professional writers. (Julie Rogers)

We are interested in models. If the organization has the ability to translate their success and reach the press, then this can be impressive. (Terry Saario)

BROCHURES

If an organization already has brochures, they should send them, since pictures can be helpful. But they shouldn't go out and create a brochure just to send to us. (Julie Rogers)

Brochures can be useful if they tell the story. But they are not helpful if the organization is just trying to impress us. Brochures should not be overdone. (Norman Brown)

Brochures are okay, but they usually overstate the case. And it can be a danger sign if the founder is in 12 out of 15 pictures. (Andrew Lark)

Brochures can sometimes be useful in conveying the sense of mission of the organization. (William Bondurant)

I don't like to see an agency spend a lot of money on glossy brochures. (Joseph Cruickshank)

Brochures can be a real indicator of the image an organization is trying to project. It's essential, however, that whatever image or tone the brochure projects, it must match the proposal. Otherwise you might question the organization's goals. (Jessica Chao)

VIDEOS

We sometimes look at them, but they can be a major pain in the neck. What do you do with them? They make the pile of mail even higher. Also, if poorly done, they can convey a bad impression. (Vincent McGee)

The written word must get our attention first. We don't encourage videos. (Norman Brown)

What is most important is the proposal. If we are really interested in a project because of a proposal, we may look at a video, particularly if it's from out of town and we can't do a site visit. They can be more valuable once we get involved with an agency. If they are sent they must be short, no more than 12 minutes. (Ilene Mack)

A video would help only if it were truly relevant to the project. But I would want to see that the expense had been underwritten. (Joyce Bove)

We have no time to look at videos. (Terry Saario, Eugene Wilson)

We get perhaps one request a year where the project could only be understood by video. They should not be sent unless that is the case. (Cynthia Mayeda)

We watch them, but it probably doesn't make a difference in funding. We get concerned if they make everything appear rosy. (Joseph Cruickshank)

Videos are costly to produce. If you have one, send it, but don't do one for us. We don't have a VCR in the office so it means that we would have to take the video home to view. (Andrew Lark)

We generally look at tapes only after reading a proposal. As a record of the grant consideration and as a means of dealing fairly with all applicants, the printed word is most important. We are much more interested in how applicants express themselves in words. Our board won't take the time to look at videos at board meetings. (William Bondurant)

It generally involves considerable effort on our part to view videos. Only submit them if they are absolutely pertinent, and we couldn't understand the project without them. (Charles Johnson)

I take them home to view. Then I look at them with a grain of salt. (Peter Calder)

ANECDOTES

I like anecdotal information and quotes a lot. They can be very powerful. But they can backfire if not relevant. It's important not to try to pull the heartstrings. (Madeline Lee)

Anecdotes are great. They make the proposal more personal. (Hildy Simmons)

Anecdotes have limited value. They don't replace an analytical approach to the problem and solution. They do have some value in making the problem more real to our board. (Joyce Bove)

Anecdotes do nothing for me....You never know the veracity. Is this just one instance or is it true of thirty? (Andrew Lark)

Anecdotal information is often persuasive, particularly when it involves human stories. It is a form of reaching out. [Anecdotes] can often be touching and compelling. (William Bondurant)

Anecdotes can make the case come alive. (Charles Johnson)

A modest use of anecdotes can help. Case histories, for instance, can give a sense of reality. But I don't like fluff. (Joseph Cruickshank)

Anecdotal information can be helpful if it illustrates the agency's capacity and track record. (Norman Brown)

Anecdotal information can be helpful at the end of the proposal. But I don't like volumes. (Ilene Mack)

I don't find anecdotes useful. We struggle with too much verbiage. (Terry Saario)

STATISTICS

A lot of statistics and graphics can be confusing. They are okay if they are concise and come to the point. (Vincent McGee)

We know the issues in our area. You don't need to tell us. If you have done some new research in a particular area, you might let us know that and mention that we can get in touch with you for the report. (Donna Dunlop)

It depends on the project. Numbers can prove anything. They are all right to use in a proposal if they are really vital. (Ilene Mack)

Statistics are important. They set the stage and give a context for the project. (Joseph Cruickshank)

Sometimes a proposal will contain a lot of irrelevant statistics. It makes one wonder why they are there. If there are relevant statistics, it is good to refer to them in the proposal, but put them in the appendix. (Charles Johnson)

Statistics can be good if they are well documented. It gives a sense that the organization is aware of other resources in the area and of an interconnectedness. (William Bondurant)

Statistics can help make the case. They show that you recognize the issue and have a knowledge of the field. It is important to show that you have an awareness of what others are doing and that you have a vision of the larger problem. I like to see that an organization realizes they are not operating in a vacuum. (Hildy Simmons)

How important is layout and presentation?

We look at the thought, not the layout, as long as the proposal can be understood. The thought can't be muddled. If the layout, bullets, etc., guide the reader in a logical progression, they can be useful. We discount some spelling errors, but if the proposal is rife with errors, of if they can't even spell my name or the name of the foundation right, then we begin to suspect that they might also be sloppy in carrying out their programs. (Andrew Lark)

Layout and presentation become a factor only when they are on the outer fringes of either being too sloppy or too slick. Then it can be distracting from the issues and ideas that are being presented. (William Bondurant)

Clarity and readability are essential. The easier the proposals are to read, the better. Language is the most important, especially the ability to present a project clearly. (Barbara Finberg)

It's important to put your best foot forward. Communicate as simply, briefly, and succinctly as possible. (Norman Brown)

The very best proposals are those that are simple and to the point. Headings are very important and can keep a proposal from becoming too dense. (Donna Dunlop)

Readability has a lot of bearing. Clarity of presentation is helpful. It is very annoying if the print is too small. (Julie Rogers)

Term paper quality is sufficient. It should be easy to read and accessible. It doesn't need a lot of bells and whistles. (Hildy Simmons)

The ideas need to stand out. If the format of the proposal helps accomplish that, then it is O.K. But fancy fonts and layout don't carry much weight in and of themselves. (Terry Saario)

Layout is very important if it makes the proposal clear and easy to read. The proposal should not be dense. When you have a huge amount of paper to go through, it helps to be able to skim the proposal quickly. (Vincent McGee)

When we look at a proposal, 50 percent of our response is objective and 50 percent is gut reaction. We once funded a proposal that was handwritten because the idea and project were so compelling. (Joseph Cruickshank)

We once funded an organization when a request was penciled on a postcard. But the idea was so clearly presented that we called to find out more information. (Vincent McGee)

How should proposals be assembled?

The presentation should be simple. A black strip binder can be useful in keeping everything together. It's good to have the proposal and appendix separated. (Joseph Cruickshank)

It should be stapled. If a proposal is bound, it is too difficult to make copies. (Julie Rogers)

Don't put the proposal in fancy books with bindings, because we take proposals apart. Stapling pages within sections is helpful. Paper clips tend to come off, or pages can get stuck to someone else's proposal. (Jessica Chao)

I hate proposals in plastic or loose leaf binders with a lot of plastic tabs and indices. It's also ecologically unsound. We have a space problem, and large packages take up even more room. (Ilene Mack)

They should be stapled or clipped. Once we receive the proposals we rearrange them. They should not be slick. Three-ring binders are terrible. I don't like to see an agency spend extra postage. It is a waste of money. (Andrew Lark)

How can a proposal writer grab and keep your attention?

Don't repeat information. Especially, don't repeat the same information in the cover letter as you have in the proposal. It is very frustrating. Organize the proposal into different sections, and be sure it has a logical layout. Be sure the program person involved reads the proposal before it is sent in. (Andrew Lark)

Stick with clarity and no fluff. I remember one proposal that was just a bullet format. It was clear, succinct and to the point. There were no adjectives. From a literary point of view it was dull, but programmatically it was clear and precise. (William Bondurant)

Provide a clear statement of the request, a clear statement of the need, and a clear statement of how the need will be met. (Joseph Cruickshank)

If it is clear, concise, and to the point, everything should be there without having to look for it. There should be meat on the bones but no fat. (Ilene Mack)

I like a proposal that respects my time. It is clear, honest and jargon free, direct, brief and well written with a minimum of puff. (Madeline Lee)

What are some red flags that can cause a proposal to be rejected?

If it doesn't meet our objectives. (Terry Saario)

First if it's not within our guidelines. Then arrogance. An attitude of "You owe us," or of "We are the only ones doing a good job. We are better than everyone else." (Vincent McGee)

If the cover letter is muddled and has lots of misspellings, it would make me wonder if the organization can put on a good program. Overstatement in the proposal is the worst thing— someone trying to pull the wool over our eyes. Keep it honest, we respect this. (Andrew Lark)

Rhetoric and puff are red flags. (Madeline Lee)

If there is something that instills a lack of confidence in the applicant's judgment. For instance, if their board of directors consists of two family members and one of these is the executive director. (William Bondurant)

A program budget which appears inflated when compared with the organization's general operating expenses. (Peter Calder)

Anything that would indicate a lack of credibility. First, if there is something outrageous in the financial statements, like 60 percent administrative costs. Or if there is a *major* shortfall in the budget. Or if the audit has a qualifying statement. We pay a lot of attention to the audit. Second, if it doesn't show that the people are capable. Third, if it's clear people have made no attempt to understand our guidelines in terms of dollars requested or the kind of project. (Joseph Cruickshank)

...lack of honesty or failure to be straightforward. (Julie Rogers)

What are some of your pet peeves?

...lack of preparation for the interview: the person who wants to talk for one hour but hasn't taken the time to read about our foundation. (William Bondurant)

People who send in their proposals by anything other than regular mail. I heard a director of a nonprofit say he had been told if they sent the proposal by overnight mail, the foundation would be impressed that they considered their project so important. That is not true here. If we get one that way that is huge, my secretary will often come in my office and say, "Look at this 37-pound proposal that was sent by Federal Express!" As a corporate foundation we are always concerned about the margin. The small margin can mean greater profits. For our foundation that means that if I am careful about the margin, I can make an extra grant that year. We expect nonprofits to be equally concerned about that margin. (Cynthia Mayeda)

We prefer to deal with the people who are carrying out the project, not the fundraisers. On occasion we have had development officers who won't let us meet with the staff people. (Norman Brown)

People who don't listen for the "no" and are pushy on the telephone. There is a fine line between being persistent and pestering. (Ilene Mack)

Having to struggle to find what the request is. Having to wade through endless discussion of the problem before getting to the proposed solution. (Jessica Chao)

People who don't understand that this is not a game. Believe what we tell you. (Joyce Bove)

Tiny print. Bound proposals. Using board connections without informing staff first. (Julie Rogers)

What makes me crazy is an organization ignoring our guidelines. Either they don't respect our guidelines about programmatic areas we fund, or they don't follow the application guidelines and don't include the materials we ask for. (Hildy Simmons)

First, people who don't read our guidelines or listen to what we tell them on the telephone. It drives me crazy when we say, "Don't submit a request," and they do anyway. Second, people who assume that funders don't have brains and try to go around the process to a board member. The staff does the work. Be respectful of the process. The foundation is more than a checkbook. Third, people who are overly academic or pompous. (Terry Saario)

First, sloppiness and misspelling of people's names. This may tick you off from the start. Second, too much paper. Third, vagueness and jargon. Fourth, the lobbying effort, such as 25 endorsement letters. (Vincent McGee)

One of the most burdensome things we have to deal with is the question from an agency: "How much should we ask for? They should have done their homework." (Eugene Wilson)

People who call to say, "What is Lilly interested in, because we want to submit?" (Charles Johnson)

Arrogance. The assumption that we will continue to support an organization. We want to solve, rather than subsidize, problems. (Eugene Wilson)

Sending a letter to my predecessor who left 13 years ago. Addressing me by my first name when I don't know you. Throw-away flattery like, "I am writing because I know of the wonderful work of your distinguished foundation...." (Madeline Lee)

If you could give one piece of advice to a grantseeker what would it be?

Check the guidelines for the foundation, and then inquire to see if they are interested in the project before spending a lot of time writing a request. (Barbara Finberg)

Find out as much as you can about the foundation. Target your approach — the rifle rather than shotgun approach. I think ten targeted proposals will have a greater chance than 100 shotgun approaches. (Ilene Mack)

Don't have your board members spend a lot of time figuring out how to get me or my trustees to a dinner party. This doesn't help. If you think your proposal is a long shot, be honest and state this right up front. If we do come to visit you, don't try to impress us. Don't buy a new suit and serve us a fancy lunch with waiters in white jackets. (Vincent McGee)

Write up a concept paper and let it rest for a week. Then look at it again and bounce if off your colleagues to test if it is clear. Get a second reader who shares your vision and ask if it really communi-

146

cates what you are trying to say. Have you communicated honestly and straightforwardly what you are trying to do? (Norman Brown)

Know yourself. Be sure you and your board have a clear statement of your mission. Be able to state why you are different and how your organization can solve problems. And do your homework about us. (Eugene Wilson)

Don't try to pull the wool over our eyes. Be honest and straightforward. (Andrew Lark)

Be thorough in your preparation and research before attempting to initiate contact with a funder. (Charles Johnson)

People give to people. So develop relationships with the foundation's program staff. This is essential. In a competitive environment we have too little money to fund too many good programs. An organization we know is more likely to get funded. (Julie Rogers)

Be honest. (Joseph Cruickshank)

Trust program officers. Don't see them as people you are trying to manipulate. (Terry Saario)

Don't pay as much attention to the rhetoric of the foundation's annual report as to their grants. You can spot changes in the foundation even before they are aware of what is going on, just by looking at their grants. This provides a window of opportunity. (Madeline Lee)

Do you see any trends in the coming years?

Larger foundations are taking more seriously the role they can play in formulating public policy; therefore, we are becoming more self-initiating. More and more often we are deciding what areas we want to investigate and then seeking out organizations to carry out these projects. The problem with this trend is that it tends to feed on itself. So we are trying still to be open-minded to requests that come across our desk so that we can be aware of trends and problems that people in the field are dealing with. Also, the area of linkages is going to become of even greater importance. We like to see researchers learning from each other and researchers and policymakers learning from each other. (Barbara Finberg)

We are looking for partners. Eighty-five percent of our grants are now foundation-initiated. This trend will only continue. As a funder, we need to keep our finger on the pulse of what is going on "out there," so we will never say we don't want to see cold proposals. But fewer of these are getting funded. Right now, only 10 percent of the proposals we receive which are within our guidelines get funded. The other trend is that there is increasing professionalization of the field. People on "this side" know a lot more about the "other side" than in the past. (Donna Dunlop)

We are trying to focus more within each of our categories. We are moving away from the smaller, community-based organizations and funding the larger, regional and national groups. In the future, we will be looking at collaboration efforts among grantseekers. We ourselves are making more collaborative grants. (Ilene Mack)

Everyone is worried about where the country is going, so a lot of foundations are doing soul searching. We will probably become even more specific in the focus of our grantmaking and intensify our commitment in those areas. (Madeline Lee)

Our board is talking about making larger grants to a fewer number of organizations in order to increase the impact of our funds. (William Bondurant)

Many foundations are becoming more focused in their grantmaking. We might try to build the capacity of a particular sector or neighborhood, for instance. There will be greater competition for grants, and guidelines will become even more important, rather than less. An organization will have to more carefully demonstrate "staying power." We will be pumping our resources into the best bets. There will be survival of the fittest. Organizations will need to think seriously about merging or coordinating with others. (Joyce Bove)

We are narrowing the issues on which we work. Competition will be heightened, so we will start to see a downsizing in the overall number of nonprofits. Those that survive will be the ones that have the capacity to really help their beneficiaries. We'll need to start looking more and more at operating support for those organizations that do survive. (Terry Saario)

We are becoming more sharply focused and less charitable. We are not in the charity business. The barrier to funds is getting higher and higher. We are becoming more isolated. Organizations will need to work harder to get around the gatekeeper. More needs and reduced staff and funds will make for increased frustration on both sides. (Eugene Wilson)

We are looking at long-term survival. And we are becoming more interested in collaboration among agencies. (Hildy Simmons)

There will be increasing emphasis on collaboration. We are putting increasingly higher priority on those that involve the "target audience" in the design of the project. Is the solution "to" people or "with" them? Who defined the problem and is proposing the solution? We are fully convinced that the solution must include the family and neighborhood level. Otherwise it is a Band-Aid. (Norman Brown)

There will be a push by grantmakers to make agencies collaborate and consolidate. While our funds are up, as are most foundation budgets, the competition has increased. In addition, we are considering targeting 20 percent of our funds to foundation-initiated areas. This will make the competition for unsolicited requests even greater. (Julie Rogers)

Increasingly, requests for support outstrip our resources. So we will do less funding of proposals that come in over the transom and more where we have a relationship. This makes it even more important to cultivate, communicate, and network with program officers. (Charles Johnson)

In summary, the three major trends identified by the funders we spoke with are: grantmaker-initiated grants, more focused giving, and emphasis on collaboration.

A knowledge of these trends will help the grantseeker prepare intelligently to meet the future. But keep in mind that trends in grantmaking are just that. They change over time. While it is important for grantseekers to be aware of them, it is equally important to acquire a sound footing in something that tends not to shift from year to year—good grantseeking. By this we mean presenting grant ideas to funders in the form of proposals that are too enticing to turn down. It is our hope that this guide has helped the reader learn to do just that.

APPENDIX B

Sample Proposal

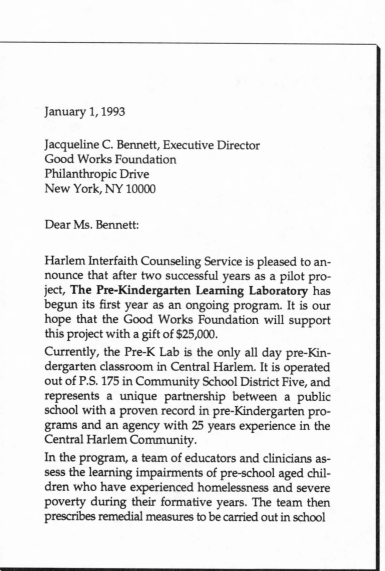

January 1, 1993

Jacqueline C. Bennett, Executive Director
Good Works Foundation
Philanthropic Drive
New York, NY 10000

Dear Ms. Bennett:

Harlem Interfaith Counseling Service is pleased to announce that after two successful years as a pilot project, **The Pre-Kindergarten Learning Laboratory** has begun its first year as an ongoing program. It is our hope that the Good Works Foundation will support this project with a gift of $25,000.

Currently, the Pre-K Lab is the only all day pre-Kindergarten classroom in Central Harlem. It is operated out of P.S. 175 in Community School District Five, and represents a unique partnership between a public school with a proven record in pre-Kindergarten programs and an agency with 25 years experience in the Central Harlem Community.

In the program, a team of educators and clinicians assess the learning impairments of pre-school aged children who have experienced homelessness and severe poverty during their formative years. The team then prescribes remedial measures to be carried out in school

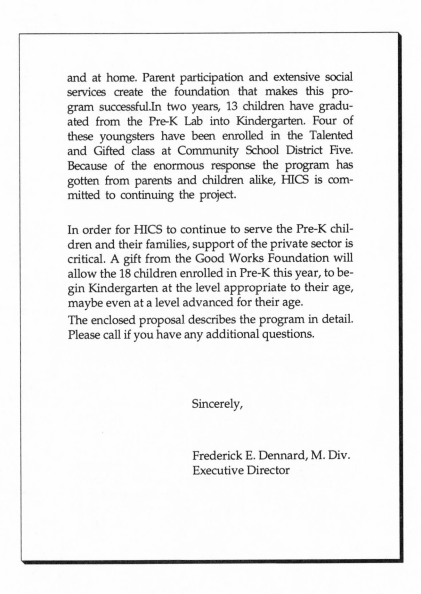

and at home. Parent participation and extensive social services create the foundation that makes this program successful.In two years, 13 children have graduated from the Pre-K Lab into Kindergarten. Four of these youngsters have been enrolled in the Talented and Gifted class at Community School District Five. Because of the enormous response the program has gotten from parents and children alike, HICS is committed to continuing the project.

In order for HICS to continue to serve the Pre-K children and their families, support of the private sector is critical. A gift from the Good Works Foundation will allow the 18 children enrolled in Pre-K this year, to begin Kindergarten at the level appropriate to their age, maybe even at a level advanced for their age.

The enclosed proposal describes the program in detail. Please call if you have any additional questions.

Sincerely,

Frederick E. Dennard, M. Div.
Executive Director

The Pre-Kindergarten Learning Laboratory: A Cooperative Educational Program for Pre-Schoolers in Central Harlem

A Proposal for Funding Submitted to Good Works Foundation

by

Harlem Interfaith Counseling Service, Inc.
215 West 125th Street
New York, New York 10027
Phone: (212)662-8613
Fax: (212)662-8667

Frederick E. Dennard, M.Div
Executive Director

TABLE OF CONTENTS

EXECUTIVE SUMMARY

Each year, over 1,000 children are born in Central Harlem. Raised in an environment of drugs, violence and urban decay, these youngsters enter public schools in Central Harlem with educational and developmental deficits that doom them to failure. Without early intervention, they will enter adolescence dependent upon public assistance or the street economy in drugs or prostitution to survive. The need for intervention is crucial. The time for action is now.

In 1989, Harlem Interfaith Counseling Service (HICS) and New York City Community School District Five began the **Pre-Kindergarten Learning Laboratory** to assess, remediate and prevent learning and developmental deficits in these preschoolers before they enter the first grade. The project's objectives are to:

- examine the nature and extent of cognitive/developmental deficits common among pre-schoolers born into poverty;

- enhance each child's capacity to participate in first grade curriculum through intervention by a team consisting of educators, psychologists, and other clinicians;

- support the child through social and clinical services designed to:

  - foster each parent's interest and involvement in their child's education; and

  - stabilize families to create the orderly, structured environment crucial to the development of a young child during his or her formative years.

The project recently completed its two-year pilot phase. Of 17 children who began the program in 1989, 13 entered kindergarten in September, 1991—four have been enrolled in a gifted and talented class! Our successes during this pilot phase have encouraged HICS and District Five schools to establish the first and only all-day pre-kindergarten classroom in Central Harlem.

The Pre-Kindergarten Learning Laboratory is not fully funded by the New York State or City Departments of Education. Therefore, HICS and District Five must turn to the private sector for financial support. We hope The McNeil Foundation will consider becoming a partner in this project through a grant of $25,000. Your support will help sponsor the 1991-92 Pre-Kindergarten Learning Laboratory class of 18 pre-schoolers.

NEED

Pre-school aged children born into poor families in Central Harlem are in jeopardy of failure in school. Denied a stable and nurturing environment most children in this community are subjected to extreme psychosocial trauma including a thriving drug trade, a spiraling rate of domestic violence, and uninhabitable living conditions *before they enter the first grade.*

These youngsters are entering our schools without crucial skills and concepts. Unless their developmental deficits are subject to early diagnosis and intervention, today's pre-schoolers are at-risk of becoming tomorrow's dysfunctional parents.

Correcting the complex psychological and educational deficiencies inherent in Central Harlem's pre-schoolers are beyond the training and abilities of the average pre-school teacher. The classroom must become an interdisciplinary laboratory where educators and clinicians interact with poor children and parents on a daily basis. Working as a team, teachers, educational psychologists, clinical social workers, psychiatrists, and family living skills counselors can:

- evaluate and promote physical, cognitive, emotional and social growth;

- help parents empower themselves to stimulate and safeguard the development of their children.

Since the fall of 1989, the Pre-Kindergarten Learning Laboratory project has given 13 children a chance for success in the classroom. This project is both appropriate and timely given the fact that:

- the majority of children attending public schools in Central Harlem are from families on public assistance;
- Central Harlem, served by Community School District Five, is a primary site for the relocation of homeless families into permanent housing;
- •currently, no funds are available for an all-day pre-kindergarten program in any District Five schools; and
- the district is experiencing the impact of the special needs of school age children who have experienced homelessness or who are still housed in congregate family shelters in the community.

Of seventeen children who entered the program in November 1989, 13 began Kindergarten in September of 1991.

Significant findings from the pilot period include:

- all children who entered the program showed language delays. Guided by the expertise of an early childhood specialist, the classroom teacher was able to develop an individualized plan for each child to remediate these delays;
- a significant number of Pre-K parents have histories of child abuse and neglect, as well as substance abuse;
- *25% of the graduating class of thirteen are gifted and talented.* These children have been enrolled in a Talented and Gifted Kindergarten class for 1991.

The final conclusion of the project leaders and staff is that the Pre-Kindergarten Learning Laboratory offers a positive means for reducing the intensity of child abuse and neglect for young children by combining effective techniques in the classroom with services designed to motivate and empower parents. This conclusion has led to the creation of the first and only all day pre-kindergarten program in Community School District Five.

PROGRAM DESCRIPTION

Goals and Objectives

The Pre-Kindergarten Learning Laboratory is conducted jointly by the Harlem Interfaith Counseling Service and Community School District Five. Its objectives are to:

- examine the nature and extent of cognitive/ development deficits common among pre-schoolers born into poor families;
- enhance each child's capacity to participate in first grade curriculum through intervention by a team consisting of educators, psychologists, and other clinicians;
- support the child through social and clinical services designed to:
    - foster each parent's interest and involvement in their child's education; and
    - stabilize families to create the orderly, structured environment crucial to the development of a young child during his or her formative years.

A maximum of 18 three-year-old children will be admitted to the Pre-Kindergarten Learning Laboratory during the 1991-1992 school year. To participate, the following criteria must be met:

- Three years old at the time of admission;
- family resides in Community School District Five;
- parent is receptive to full participation of self and child in all Pre-Kindergarten Learning Laboratory activities, including Parent Training;
- current Medical Report documents that the child is free from all contagious diseases and has had all required immunization.

Methodology

Each parent and child will go through the following procedures during their involvement with the program.

Screening Process

Every parent and child referred for the Pre-Kindergarten Learning Laboratory meets with a HICS Senior Clinical Social Worker who functions as the Treatment Team Facilitator. A therapeutic screening process includes the gathering of extensive pre and postnatal history on the child's development, a thorough medical and immunizations history, and a complete psychosocial history on the family.

Program Admission

It will be the responsibility of the Treatment Team Facilitator to explain the objectives, requirements, and program content of the Pre-Kindergarten Learning Laboratory in a manner which enables the parent to make an informed decision to participate in the two year process. When the parent has accepted all conditions and has signed the application, the Team Facilitator arranges an introduction to the Parent Support Team.

Each child will have a thorough Diagnostic Learning Evaluation upon entering the Pre-Kindergarten Learning Laboratory. The evaluation will document the cognitive and developmental deficits exhibited and will consist of three separate evaluations:

Neurosensory Evaluation:

The visual and auditory systems are the primary channels of learning. To evaluate the child's capacity to use these systems, each child will be referred to the Developmental Evaluation Unit of Sydenham Neighborhood Family Care Center for a comprehensive speech and language, visual and auditory assessment.

Cognitive Skills Assessment:

Various standardized instruments, including the Kaufman Assessment Battery for Children (K-ABC), are used by the psychologist to evaluate the child's cognitive and perceptual/motor abilities, as well as the development of age appropriate basic concepts. Particular emphasis will be given to those skills necessary for successful participation in first grade curriculum.

Behavioral Observations:

Each child will be observed to assess social interactive skills, ability to follow directions, intellectual curiosity, coping strategies and interaction with the parent. Over a two-year period, the child will be observed at specific intervals to measure growth.

At the conclusion of a child's stay in the program, a similar in-depth evaluation will be conducted to determine his or her learning needs in preparation for admission to District Five Kindergarten. So that staff may continually assess program impact, this data will also be compared to the admissions data and to the extent possible to a small sample of children of similar history who have not participated in a therapeutic day-care process.

Problems identified through The Diagnostic Learning Evaluation will form the basis for an Individual Remediation Plan. This plan will be developed in consultation with the teacher and parent(s) and will outline specific goals for the child. Furthermore, the Plan will describe steps to be taken both in the classroom and at home. Periodic post-testing will be conducted to monitor the child's progress and the need for modification in the plan.

Individualized Educational Plan for Program Graduates

An educational plan for each program graduate will be developed jointly by HICS, the teachers of District Five and the parents. For the first year, follow-up interviews with the kindergarten teachers and classroom observations will occur at regular intervals. Those children who continue to manifest symptoms of learning or adjustment difficulties will be monitored more closely. Follow-up and observations will continue through the first grade. At the conclusion of the first grade, the children will be reevaluated for academic progress as compared to other first graders.

Parent Support Training

The Early Childhood Education Specialist conducts training sessions for parents on an individual and group basis. The goal is to help parents develop teaching activities to use with their child at home. Sessions combine the demonstration of the activity by the psychologist and observation of the parent and child engaging in the activity with appropriate feedback. Topics include but are not limited to the following:

- designing educational activities around common everyday experiences, e.g. naming, categorizing, describing, re-telling;
- making inexpensive educational toys;
- parents' role as partners in the educational process;
- child management techniques—discipline without tears.

Parent and Family Support Services

Stability in the home is crucial for a positive experience in the Pre-Kindergarten Learning Laboratory. Following admission to the program, immediate steps must be taken to enable the parent and family to be able to participate effectively with the child.

The basic philosophy of HICS' services is that to treat the individual, treatment must be made available to the family. Experience in serving families in Central Harlem has taught us that in addition to the developmental needs of each pre-schooler, his or her family will have a variety of highly complex clinical, social, and case management needs. Therefore, a target population of 18 pre-school youngsters is the caseload equivalent of 90 persons, including a minimum of 18 parents and 54 school-age siblings. To effectively deal with this caseload, Parent Support Teams and Family

Treatment Teams target specific needs and collaborate to meet them.

A Clinical Social Worker and the Family Living Skills Counselor form the Parent Support Team. This team works in the classroom, field and agency to provide the instruction and resources necessary to ensure the parent and child's consistent and effective participation in the Pre-Kindergarten Learning Laboratory.

The Parent Support Team will conduct an Admission Readiness Assessment in the client's home and in the office. This assessment will identify existing and potential deficiencies in parenting and educational skills. Results will be used by the team and each parent to develop an Individualized Parent Preparation Plan which outlines specific steps to be taken to overcome these deficiencies. At this time, the Team and the parent agree upon a specific timetable for implementation.

Staffing

The success of the Pre-K Lab is contingent upon the expertise of HICS staff. Project staff must not only have a strong educational background, but experience in working with the highly resistant population that HICS serves as well. Each staff member must be able to work well with colleagues in other disciplines as part of the Family Treatment Team.

A Family Treatment Team consisting of the Treatment Team Facilitator (Clinical Social Worker) and a Family Living Skills Counselor, will be assigned to each family. Classroom activities will be conducted by a Teacher, with the help of a Teacher's Aid. The program also uses a number of consultants to carry out specific aspects of the program. These consultants include, a Testing psychologist to perform screening and follow up testing with the help of a Training Psychologist. In addition, an Early Childhood Specialist will conduct training sessions for parents and help formulate educational plans for students.

Administration

The Treatment Team Facilitator will communicate and network with all persons involved in the Project and expedite treatment services for family members at HICS. The Team will also make appropriate referrals and follow-ups to community based medical services and other community based services which may be needed by these families.

Evaluation

On a continuing basis, data is being collected on the developmental deficits of Pre-Kindergarten Learning Laboratory students as well as the results of early intervention with prescriptive remediation, parent training, and the provision of social and clinical services to the families. Measurable data includes, but will not be limited to: student attendance, parent attendance at training sessions, and test scores. Written and oral responses from student and parent participants and behavioral observations will help educators and clinicians gauge the effectiveness of the program.

Findings are analyzed to examine:

- the nature and extent of cognitive/developmental deficits common among pre-schoolers whose families have a history of dependence on public assistance;
- the impact of early prescriptive remedial intervention on the child's capacity to participate in first grade curriculum;
- the impact of providing social and clinical services to parents and siblings no the child's development;
- the results of a joint initiative by a community school district and a community-based mental health clinic cooperatively serving poor families with pre-school age children.

ORGANIZATIONAL INFORMATION

Founded in 1966, **Harlem Interfaith Counseling Service, Inc., (HICS)**, is a voluntary outpatient family mental health clinic. The agency is licensed by the Office of Mental Health of the New York State Department of Mental Hygiene and serves clients regardless of ethnicity or economic status.

Prevention, as well as treatment, of acute symptoms form the core of agency services. HICS's service philosophy is based upon an ecostructural family treatment approach including: family, individual and group verbal therapies; task and skills training; and social therapy groups.

In 1988, HICS initiated the *Family and Youth Support System* (FYSS), a comprehensive program designed to empower recently rehoused families in Central Harlem to achieve self-sufficiency, therefore avoiding a return to homelessness. HICS' clinicians, social workers and family living skills counselors provide task and skill training and psychosocial services needed to help families make creative adjustments to living in a new community and to enable them to learn life management skills to function outside of a hotel and shelter system.

Community School District Five has taken the leadership in early childhood education for five years, and conducts a model pre-kindergarten program. In 1982, before categorical funding was available for all day kindergarten, District Five allocated precious tax levy funds for all day kindergartens for four-year-olds in every District Five elementary school. In 1983-84, the District Five finally received State Pre-Kindergarten funds for the first time, and established a district-wide program at P.S. 36. Currently, no funds are available for an all day pre-kindergarten program in any District Five school.

District Five offers unusually modern facilities designed for effective early childhood education. Administrators and educators from District Five, experienced in maintaining a quality model program in pre-kindergarten education, will work closely with professional staff from Harlem Interfaith Counseling Service to provide a nurturing educational environment for students.

CONCLUSION

Thousands of poor, homeless or formerly homeless pre-schoolers are entering our schools. Early evaluation of their needs and immediate intervention is crucial. The result will be the remediation of physical, cognitive, emotional and social deficits which leave them at-risk even before entering the first grade.

The partnership of Community School District Five, with a proven record in pre-kindergarten education, and Harlem Interfaith Counseling Service, which is responsible for the direct delivery of services to re-housed homeless families in Central Harlem, could not come at a more critical time. In the face of an escalating number of families who live at or below the poverty level in our community of Central Harlem, the Pre-Kindergarten Learning Laboratory offers our educators and clinicians a rare opportunity. Here, we are able to reverse developmental shortfalls before they place the child in danger of academic failure.

PROJECT BUDGET
EXPENSE

Personnel Services

Senior Clinical Social Worker	$37,080
ClinicalSocial Worker	28,000
Family Living Skills Counselors (3)	66,000
Classroom Teacher	42,000
Teachers Aide (Paraprofessional)	15,000
Secretary	20,000
Subtotal:	$208,080
Consultants:	
Testing Psychologist	$21,100
Early Childhood Education Specialist	22,122
P/T Training Psychologist	39,476
Subtotal:	$82,698
Fringe Benefits (22%)	$45,778
Total Personnel Services:	$336,556
Non-Personnel Services	
Testing Supplies	$2,400
Educational Materials & Equipment	2,400
Program & Office Supplies	6,000
Transportation: Bus Rental	73,480
Staff Travel	2,100
Telephone & Postage	3,600
Subtotal:	$89,980
Administrative Overhead (10%)	$42,654
Total Non-Pers. Services:	$132,634
TOTAL BUDGETED EXPENDITURE	$469,189
INCOME	
NYC Department of Mental Health	$191,336
NYS Office of Mental Health	80,480
Private Contributions	197,373
TOTAL ANTICIPATED INCOME	**$469,189**

BUDGET NARRATIVE

The New York City Department of Mental Health and the New York State Office of Mental Health are committed to the Pre-Kindergarten Learning Laboratory and have been ongoing supporters of the project. Harlem Interfaith Counseling Service conducts extensive, ongoing outreach to foundations, corporations and individuals to secure funding for the program.

APPENDIX C

Selected Readings on Proposal Development

Compiled by Elizabeth McKenty and Sarah Collins

Especially recommended for the novice grantseeker:

Brooklyn In Touch Information Center. *Fundraising with Proposals.* Brooklyn, N.Y. (1 Hanson Pl., Room 2504, 11243): Brooklyn In Touch Information Center, 1988. 13 p. ($5)
> Basic guide for the novice fundraiser. Includes an introductory article—"How to Know Your Grantmaker"—on how to begin research on funding sources, tables, lists of fundraising turn-offs, as well as a sample proposal outline and a cover letter.

Burns, Michael E. *Proposal Writer's Guide.* Hartford, Conn. (30 Arbor Street, 06106): D.A.T.A., 1989. 35 p. ($12.95)

Step-by-step approach to preparing written fund
requests. Includes two sample proposals.

Coggins, Christiana. *A User's Guide to Proposal Writing: Or How to
Get Your Project Funded.* New York (902 Broadway, 10010): Inter-
national Planned Parenthood Federation/Western Hemisphere
Region, Inc., 1990. 17 p. ($10)
> Primarily intended for use in submitting a proposal
> to the Planned Parenthood Federation, this brief
> how-to guide is divided into the eight components
> of a proposal. Concludes with a useful sample
> proposal. Also available in Spanish.

Conrad, Daniel Lynn. *The Quick Proposal Workbook.* San Francisco
(358 Brannan Street, 94107): Public Management Institute, 1980.
117 p.
> A workbook on project planning, proposal writing,
> and evaluation techniques.

Kiritz, Norton J. *Program Planning and Proposal Writing: Expanded
Version.* Grantsmanship Center Reprint Series on Program Planning & Proposal Writing. Los Angeles: Grantsmanship Center,
1980. 47 p. ($4)
> Step-by-step guide to a widely-used format in clear,
> concise language.

For more advanced fundraisers:

Belcher, Jane C., and Julia M. Jacobsen. *From Idea to Funded Project: Grant Proposals that Work.* 4th ed., rev. Phoenix, Ariz. (2214
North Central, 85004-1483): Oryx Press, 1992. v, 138 p. ($19.95)
> Presents a method for nurturing an idea from
> inception through the process of developing a
> proposal, finding sources of support, administering
> grants, and evaluation. Second part provides
> information on basic resources and reprints several
> forms and regulations for government funding
> sources.

Bowman, Joel P., and Bernardine P. Branchaw. *How to Write Proposals that Produce.* Phoenix, Ariz. (2214 North Central, 85004-
1483): Oryx Press, 1992. xii, 236 p. ($23)

Detailed and technical treatment of the process of
writing proposals. Geared toward both business and
nonprofit organizations.

Browning, Beverly A. *Successful Grant Writing Tips: The Manual.*
Burton, Mich. (4355 South Saginaw Street, 48529): Grantsline
Inc., 1991. iii, 91 p. ($39.95)
Covers each element of a proposal, complete with
examples, tables, and graphics.

Coley, Soraya M., and Cynthia A. Scheinberg. *Proposal Writing.*
Sage Human Services Guides, no. 63. Newbury Park, Calif. (2455
Teller Road, 91320): Sage Publications, 1990. 130 p. ($14.95)
Intended primarily for the moderately experienced
grantseeker, this guide provides step-by-step advice
for developing proposals. Examples and worksheets
throughout.

Gooch, Judith Mirick. *Writing Winning Proposals.* Washington (11
Dupont Circle, Suite 400, 20036): Council for Advancement and
Support of Education, 1987. vii, 87 p. ($27.00)
Focuses primarily on college and university
proposal writing, but provides general information
useful to all grantseekers. Detailed—includes a case
study, samples, and a bibliography.

Hall, Mary S. *Getting Funded: A Complete Guide to Proposal Writing.*
3rd ed. Portland, Oreg. (P.O. Box 1491, 97207): Continuing Education Press, 1988. viii, 206 p. ($19.95)
This soup-to-nuts guidebook is organized along a
logical pattern of planning. Each chapter of the
section dealing with the actual writing of a proposal
focuses on a specific component. Includes resource
lists, cases, models, checklists, and sample formats.

Kalish, Susan Ezell, ed. *The Proposal Writer's Swipe File: 15 Winning Fund-Raising Proposals...Prototypes of Approaches, Styles, and
Structures.* 3rd ed. Rockville, Md. (12300 Twinbrook Parkway,
Suite 450, 20852): Taft Group, 1984. viii, 162 p. ($21.95)
Contains fifteen complete sample proposals, written
by education, science, and arts and humanities
organizations to foundations or corporate giving
programs.

Lauffer, Armand. *Grantsmanship.* 2nd ed. Beverly Hills, Calif.: Sage Publications, 1983. 120 p. ($15.95)

> Practical workbook for developing a fundraising/marketing strategy, identifying funding sources, and developing a budget and proposal.

Lefferts, Robert B. *Getting a Grant in the 1990s: How to Write Successful Grant Proposals.* New York (15 Columbus Circle, 10023): Prentice Hall Press, 1990. xiii, 239 p. ($12.95)

> Manual provides guidelines for preparing, writing, and presenting proposals to foundations and government agencies. Intended for those seeking funding for human services. Includes a critiqued sample program proposal, a glossary, and annotated bibliographies.

Meador, Roy. *Guidelines for Preparing Proposals.* 2nd ed. Chelsea, Mich. (121 South Main Street, 48118): Lewis Publishers, 1991. xiii, 204 p. ($24.95)

> Advanced manual on proposals for business, government, and foundations. The book contains the usual guidelines for a proposal but with the additional guidelines necessary for use in a highly technical or scientific project.

White, Virginia P., ed. *Grant Proposals that Succeeded.* Nonprofit Management and Finance. New York: Plenum, 1984. viii, 240 p. ($32.50)

> Presents proposals that originally appeared in *Grants Magazine,* and covers research grants, training grants, arts applications, humanities (describing the grantmaking process of the National Endowment for the Humanities), and a response to a request for proposal.

APPENDIX D

Publications and Services of the Foundation Center

The Foundation Center is a national service organization founded and supported by foundations to provide a single authoritative source of information on foundation and corporate giving. The Center's programs are designed to help grantseekers as they begin to select those funders that may be most interested in their projects from the over 33,000 active U.S. foundations. Among its primary activities toward this end are publishing reference books on foundation and corporate philanthropy and disseminating information on grantmaking through a nation-wide public service program.

Publications of the Foundation Center are the primary working tools of every serious grantseeker. They are also used by grantmakers, scholars, journalists, and legislators, in short, by everyone seeking any type of factual information on philan-thropy. All private foundations and a significant number of cor-porations actively engaged in grantmaking, regardless of size or geographic location, are included in one or more of the Center's publications. The publications are of three kinds: directories that describe specific funders, characterizing their program interests and providing fiscal and personnel data; grants indexes that list and classify by subject recent foundation and corporate awards; and guides, monographs, and bibliographies that introduce the reader to funding research, elements of proposal writing, and nonprofit management issues. The majority of the reference titles are updated annually. The publishing information that follows describes the editions current at the time of initial publication.

Foundation Center publications may be ordered from the Foundation Center, 79 Fifth Avenue, New York, NY 10003-3076. For more information about any aspect of the Center's program or for the name of the Center's library collection nearest you, call (800) 424-9836.

DIRECTORIES OF GRANTMAKERS

THE FOUNDATION DIRECTORY, 1993 Edition

The Foundation Directory has been widely known and respected in the field for over 30 years. It includes the latest information on all foundations whose assets exceed $2 million or whose annual grants total $200,000 or more. The 1993 Edition includes more than 6,300 of these foundations, 400 of which are new to this edition. *Directory* foundations hold $151 billion in assets and award $8 billion in grants annually, accounting for 90 percent of all U.S. foundation dollars awarded in 1991.

Each *Directory* entry contains precise information on applica-tion procedures, giving limitations, types of support awarded, the publications of each foundation, and foundation staff. In addition, each entry features information on the grantmakers' giving interests, financial data, grant amounts, addresses, and telephone numbers. The Foundation Center works closely with foundations to ensure the accuracy and timeliness of the infor-mation provided.

The *Directory* includes indexes by foundation name; subject areas of interest; names of donors, trustees, and officers; geographic location; and the types of support awarded. Also included are analyses of the foundation community by geography, asset and grant size, and the different foundation types.

March 1993.
Softbound: ISBN 0-87954-449-6/$160
Hardbound: ISBN 0-87954-484-8/$185
Published annually.

THE FOUNDATION DIRECTORY SUPPLEMENT

The Foundation Directory Supplement provides the latest information on *Foundation Directory* grantmakers six months after the *Directory* is published.

September 1993/ISBN 0-87954-500-3/$110

THE FOUNDATION DIRECTORY PART 2: A Guide to Grant Programs $50,000–$200,000, 1993 (2nd) Edition

The Foundation Directory Part 2 covers the next largest set of foundations, those with grant programs between $50,000 and $200,000. It includes *Directory*-level information on mid-sized foundations. Essential data on 4,327 foundations is included along with over 30,000 recently awarded foundation grants. Access to foundation entries is facilitated by five indexes organized by city and state; donors, officers, and trustees; types of support; foundation names; and over 200 specific subject areas.

March 1993/ISBN 0-87954-489-9/$160
Published biennially.

GUIDE TO U.S. FOUNDATIONS, THEIR TRUSTEES, OFFICERS, AND DONORS

This provides fundraisers with current, accurate information on all 33,000+ active grantmaking foundations in the United States. The two-volume set also includes a master list of the names of the people who establish, oversee, and manage those institutions. Each entry includes asset and giving amounts as well as geographic limitations.

This guide includes over 20,000 grantmakers not covered in other Foundation Center publications. Each entry also tells you if you can find more extensive information on the grantmaker in another Foundation Center reference work.

March 1993/0-87954-488-0/$195

THE FOUNDATION 1000

The Foundation 1000 provides access to extensive and accurate information on the largest grantmakers, which together distribute over 60 percent of all foundation grant dollars. *Foundation 1000* grantmakers hold over $100 billion in assets and each year award nearly $6 billion, more than 190,000 grants, to nonprofit organizations nationwide.

The Foundation 1000 provides thorough analyses of the 1,000 largest foundations and their extensive grant programs. Each multipage foundation profile features a full foundation portrait, a detailed breakdown of the foundation's grant program, and many examples of recently awarded foundation grants.

There are five indexes: foundation name, subject field, type of support, and geographic location. A special new index locates grantmakers by the names of officers, donors, and trustees.

October 1993/ISBN 0-87954-503-8/$225
Published annually.

NATIONAL DIRECTORY OF CORPORATE GIVING, 3rd Edition

The 3rd Edition of the *National Directory of Corporate Giving* offers authoritative information on approximately 2,300 corporate foundations and direct giving programs.

The *National Directory* features detailed portraits of 1,700 corporate foundations plus an additional 600 direct giving programs, including application information, key personnel, types of support generally awarded, giving limitations, financial data, and purpose and activities statements. Over 1,100 entries in the 3rd Edition also include sample grants. The volume also provides data on the corporations that sponsor foundations and those that have direct giving programs. Each entry gives the company's name and address, a review of the types of business, financial data complete with Forbes and Fortune ratings, all plants and subsidiaries, and a charitable giving statement.

The *National Directory* also features an extensive bibliography to guide you to further research on corporate funding. Six indexes help you target funding prospects by geographic region;

types of support funded; subject area; officers, donors, and trustees; types of business; and names of the corporation, its foundation, and direct giving program.

October 1993/ISBN 0-87954-485-6/$195

CORPORATE FOUNDATION PROFILES, 7th Edition

This volume includes comprehensive information on 247 of the largest corporate foundations in the United States, grantmakers that each give at least $1.25 million annually. Each profile covers foundation giving interests, application guidelines, recently awarded grants, information on the sponsoring company, and many other essential fundraising facts. Three indexes help grantseekers search for prospective funders by subject area, geographic region, and types of support preferred by the foundation.

March 1992/ISBN 0-87954-437-6/$135
Published biennially.

NEW YORK STATE FOUNDATIONS: A Comprehensive Directory, 3rd Edition

This volume will help fundraisers to identify the giving interests and funding policies of over 5,200 foundations in New York State. Entries have been drawn from the most current sources of information available, including IRS 990-PF foundation tax returns and, in many cases, the foundations themselves. Many include descriptions of recently awarded grants. A separate section covers several out-of-state grantmakers that fund nonprofits in New York State. Five indexes offer quick access to foundations according to their fields of interest; types of support awarded; city and county; names of donors, officers, and trustees; and foundation names.

June 1993/ISBN 0-87954-501-1/$165.
Published biennially.

FOUNDATION GRANTS TO INDIVIDUALS, 8th Edition

The 8th Edition of this volume provides full descriptions of the programs of over 2,250 foundations, all of which award grants to individuals. Entries include foundation addresses and telephone numbers, financial data, giving limitations, and application guidelines.

April 1993/ISBN 0-87954-493-7/$55

SUBJECT DIRECTORIES

NATIONAL GUIDE TO FUNDING IN AGING,
3rd Edition

The *National Guide to Funding in Aging* covers the many public and private sources of funding support and technical assistance for programs for the aging. The 3rd Edition of this volume provides essential facts on over 1,000 grantmakers, including federal funding programs; state government funding programs (with up-to-date listings for all 50 states and U.S. territories); foundations that have demonstrated or expressed an interest in the field (many foundation entries include lists of actual recently awarded grants); plus other academic, religious, and service agencies that provide funding and technical aid to aging-related nonprofits.

December 1992/ISBN 0-87954-444-9/$80

AIDS FUNDING: A Guide to Giving by Foundations and Charitable Organizations, 3rd Edition

This volume covers over 500 foundations, corporate giving programs, and public charities that have recently awarded over $97 million for AIDS- and HIV-related nonprofit organizations involved in direct relief, medical research, legal aid, preventative education, and other programs to empower persons with AIDS and AIDS-related diseases. Grants lists accompany over half of the entries.

November 1993/ISBN 0-87954-507-0/$75

NATIONAL GUIDE TO FUNDING IN ARTS AND CULTURE,
2nd Edition

The 2nd Edition of this subject guide covers those foundations and corporate giving programs that have demonstrated a commitment to funding art colonies, dance companies, museums, theaters, and many other types of arts and culture projects and institutions. With over 4,200 grantmakers listed, six indexes, and a special bibliography, the volume facilitates rapid and accurate research. The 2nd Edition also lists thousands of actual grants recently awarded by many foundations, to show the kinds of projects currently receiving support from grantmakers.

May 1992/ISBN 0-87954-442-2/$125

NATIONAL GUIDE TO FUNDING FOR CHILDREN, YOUTH, AND FAMILIES, 2nd Edition

The 2nd Edition of this guide covers 3,000 foundations and corporate direct giving programs that together award millions of dollars each year to organizations committed to causes involving children, youth, and families. Each entry includes the grantmaker's address and contact name, purpose statement, and application guidelines.There are descriptions of over 8,000 sample grants recently awarded by many of these foundations. Six indexes help grantmakers target appropriate sources of funding, and a bibliography facilitates further research in the field.

April 1993/ISBN 0-87954-491-0/$135

NATIONAL GUIDE TO FUNDING FOR THE ECONOMICALLY DISADVANTAGED

This volume covers 1,000 foundations and corporate direct giving programs, each with a history of awarding grant dollars to projects and institutions that aid the economically disadvantaged in the areas of employment programs, homeless shelters, hunger relief, welfare initiatives, and hundreds of other subject categories.

This guide features portraits that include the grantmaker's address, financial data, giving priorities statement, application procedures, contact names, and key officials. Many entries include descriptions of over 2,000 actual grants recently awarded by the foundation or corporate giver.

May 1993/ISBN 0-87954-494-5/$85

NATIONAL GUIDE TO FUNDING FOR ELEMENTARY AND SECONDARY EDUCATION, 2nd Edition

This guide covers over 1,600 foundations and corporate direct giving programs committed to funding nursery schools, bilingual education initiatives, gifted programs, remedial reading/math, drop-out prevention services, educational testing programs and many other nonprofit organizations and activities. The volume also includes over 4,500 descriptions of recently awarded grants.

June 1993/ISBN 0-87954-495-3/$135

NATIONAL GUIDE TO FUNDING FOR THE ENVIRONMENT AND ANIMAL WELFARE

This volume offers entries on foundations and includes lists of environmental grants recently awarded to projects and organizations involved in international conservation, ecological research, litigation and advocacy, waste reduction, animal welfare, and much more. The *Guide* provides foundation addresses, financial data, giving priorities, application procedures, contact names, and key officials; sample grants; and a range of helpful indexes that help fundraisers target funders by specific program areas and geographic preferences.

April 1992/ISBN 0-87954-440-6/$75

NATIONAL GUIDE TO FUNDING IN HEALTH, 3rd Edition

The 3rd Edition of this volume covers more than 3,000 foundations and corporate direct giving programs, all of which have a documented or stated interest in funding hospitals, universities, research institutes, community-based agencies, national health associations, and a broad range of other health-related programs and services. This source includes facts on grantmakers' program interests, contact persons, application guidelines, and listings of board members. Many entries include descriptions of recently awarded grants—the volume features over 8,000 sample grants in all. Six indexes help fundraisers quickly target prospective grant sources. A bibliography of publications on health issues and philanthropic initiatives in the field is included as a guide to further study.

April 1993/ISBN 0-87954-490-2/$135

NATIONAL GUIDE TO FUNDING IN HIGHER EDUCATION, 2nd Edition

The 2nd Edition of this guide covers over 3,650 foundations and corporate giving programs, all with a proven history of awarding grants to colleges, universities, graduate programs, and research institutes. Each entry gives a thorough portrait of the grantmaker, including the address, name of the contact person, financial data, purpose statement, types of support preferred, and geographic limitations. The book includes over 13,400 descriptions of recently awarded grants. The 2nd Edition also includes a selected bibliography to direct further research on higher education and philanthropy.

May 1992/ISBN 0-87954-443-0/$125

GUIDE TO FUNDING FOR INTERNATIONAL AND FOREIGN PROGRAMS

In the *Guide to Funding for International and Foreign Programs* many of the foundation entries include lists of grants recently awarded by grantmakers to projects with an international focus, both within the United States and abroad: international relief, conferences, disaster assistance, human rights, civil liberties, community development, and education. The *Guide* provides all the facts fundraisers need to bolster their target list of funding prospects: foundation addresses, financial data, giving priorities, application procedures, contact names, and key officials; sample grants; and a range of indexes that help fundraisers target funders by specific program areas funded and geographic preferences.

May 1992/ISBN 0-87954-441-4/$75

NATIONAL GUIDE TO FUNDING FOR LIBRARIES AND INFORMATION SERVICES, 2nd Edition

The 2nd Edition of this volume covers over 400 foundations and corporate direct giving programs. Each entry includes grant-maker facts such as the address, name of the contact person, financial data, purpose statement, types of support preferred, and geographic limitations. This guide also features over 800 descriptions of recently awarded grants. This volume affords data on funders of a wide range of organizations and projects, from the smallest public libraries to major research institutions, as well as academic/research libraries, art, law, and medical libraries, and other specialized information centers.

May 1993/ISBN 0-87954-497-X/$85

NATIONAL GUIDE TO FUNDING IN RELIGION, 2nd Edition

The 2nd Edition of this guide covers over 3,000 foundations and corporate direct giving programs, all of which have demonstrated or stated an interest in funding churches, missionary societies, and/or religious welfare and religious education programs. The guide features portraits that include the grant-maker's address, financial data, giving priorities statement, application procedures, contact names, and key officials. Many entries include descriptions of actual grants recently awarded by the foundation or corporate giver. The volume includes over 3,600 sample grants.

June 1993/ISBN 0-87954-496-1/$135

NATIONAL GUIDE TO FUNDING FOR WOMEN AND GIRLS, 2nd Edition

The 2nd Edition of this guide covers over 800 foundations and corporate direct giving programs, all of which have demonstrated or stated an interest in funding such projects as education scholarships, shelters for abused women, girls' clubs, health clinics, employment centers, and other diverse programs. The guide features portraits that include the grantmaker's address, financial data, giving priorities statement, application procedures, contact names, and key officials. Many entries include descriptions of actual grants recently awarded by the foundation or corporate giver. The volume includes over 3,000 sample grants.

May 1993/ISBN 0-87954-498-8/$95

GRANT DIRECTORIES

GRANT GUIDES

Grant Guides list actual foundation grants in 30 key areas of grantmaking. These research tools show thousands of grants of $10,000 or more, all of them recently awarded by many of the top funders in each field. Each volume includes the names, addresses, and giving limitations of all foundations listed. The grant descriptions provide the grant recipient's name and location, the grant amount, and date it was authorized; and a description of the grant's intended use.

Each *Grant Guide* provides three indexes by: the type of organization generally funded by the grantmaker, the subject focus of the foundation's grants, and the geographic area in which the foundation has already funded projects. The introduction to each volume uses a series of statistical tables to document (1) the 25 top funders in your area of interest (by total dollar amount of grants), (2) the 15 largest grants reported, (3) the total dollar amount and number of grants awarded for specific types of support, recipient organization type, and population group, and (4) total grant dollars received in each U.S. state and many foreign countries.

Series published annually in September/1993/1994 Editions/$65 each

THE FOUNDATION GRANTS INDEX ANNUAL, 1994 Edition

The 1994 (22nd) Edition of *The Foundation Grants Index* covers the grantmaking programs of over 950 of the largest independent, corporate, and community foundations in the U.S. and includes over 60,000 grant descriptions in all. Grant descriptions are divided into 28 broad subject areas such as health, higher education, and arts and culture. Within each of these broad fields, the grant descriptions are listed geographically by state and alphabetically by the name of the foundation. The grant descriptions provide fundraisers with the grant recipient's name and location, the grant amount, and date it was authorized; and a description of the grant's intended use.

December 1993/ISBN 0-87954-508-9/$135

THE FOUNDATION GRANTS INDEX QUARTERLY

This subscription service provides new information on foundation funding every three months. Each issue of the *Quarterly* covers descriptions of over 5,000 recent foundation grants, arranged by state and indexed by subjects and recipients. The *Quarterly* contains updates on grantmakers that note changes in foundation address, personnel, program interests, and application procedures. Also included is a list of grantmakers' recent publications such as annual reports, information brochures, grants lists, and newsletters.

Annual subscription $85/4 issues ISSN 0735-2522

WHO GETS GRANTS / WHO GIVES GRANTS: Nonprofit Organizations and the Foundation Grants They Received

Who Gets Grants provides direct access to grant recipient information, featuring over 16,000 nonprofit organizations and more than 48,000 grants. The book is divided into 19 different subject headings. Within each subject area the grant recipients are listed by geographic area.

The grant recipient entries feature grant descriptions that include the grant amount, its duration and use, and the name of the grantmaker. An index provides a list of all the grants made by each foundation covered, which gives a sense of a grantmaker's larger funding priorities. An appendix lists foundation addresses and funding limitations.

March 1993/ISBN 0-87954-487-2/$95

RESEARCH HANDBOOKS

FOUNDATION FUNDAMENTALS: A Guide for Grantseekers, 4th Edition
Edited by Judith B. Margolin

This comprehensive guidebook presents the facts you need to understand the world of foundations, and to identify foundation funding sources for your organization. Illustrations take you step-by-step through the funding research process, and worksheets and check lists are provided to help you get started in your search for funding. Comprehensive bibliographies and detailed research examples are also supplied.

March 1991/ISBN 0-87954-392-2/$19.95

THE FOUNDATION CENTER'S USER-FRIENDLY GUIDE: Grantseeker's Guide to Resources
Edited by Judith B. Margolin

This book answers the most commonly asked questions about grantseeking in an upbeat, easy-to-read style. Specifically designed for novice grantseekers, the *User-Friendly Guide* leads the reader through the maze of unfamiliar jargon and the wide range of research guides used successfully by professional fundraisers.

February 1992/ISBN 0-87954-452-X/$12.95

FOUNDATION GIVING: Yearbook of Facts and Figures on Private, Corporate and Community Foundations, 1993 Edition

Foundation Giving includes data on more than 33,000 grantmaking foundations in the country. Using a range of statistical tables to chart foundation giving by subject area and type of support, to categorize foundations by asset and giving amount, and to document other noteworthy data such as the breakdown of grants awarded by the 100 largest foundations, the study offers a comprehensive review of foundation activity collected and analyzed over the past year.

July 1993/ISBN 0-87954-504-6/$19.95

BENCHMARK STUDIES

AGING: The Burden Study on Foundation Grantmaking Trends

This in-depth analysis of foundation funding for programs that benefit the elderly covers private, corporate, and community grantmakers and considers such pertinent topics as the availability of support for care-givers, the frail elderly, and Alzheimer's patients; a renewed interest in support services and institutional long-term care; and intergenerational programs.

September 1991/ISBN 0-87954-389-2/$40

ALCOHOL AND DRUG ABUSE FUNDING: An Analysis of Foundation Grants 1983–1987

This report provides an authoritative study of independent, corporate, and community foundation grants awarded between 1983 and 1987 for drug and alcohol abuse programs. The study examines the historical background, present status, and future directions of grantmaking in this critical field. It is designed for foundation policymakers, grantseekers, and researchers in the fields of health care and prevention, education, and social service.

August 1989/ISBN 0-87954-286-1/$45

ARTS FUNDING: A Report on Foundation and Corporate Grantmaking Trends

This comprehensive report, commissioned by Grantmakers in the Arts, documents notable shifts in arts and culture funding patterns through the 1980s. The study covers funding for the performing and visual arts, museums, ethnic arts, media, journalism, historic preservation, and arts-related humanities. *Arts Funding* features profiles of over 60 top foundation and corporate grantmakers that identify their current funding priorities. The study incorporates findings from a 1992 survey in which grantmakers predict funding directions within the field for the

1990s. *Arts Funding* also features case studies of grantmakers that have undergone dynamic change in their arts funding policy over the last two years.

March 1993/ISBN 0-87954-448-1/$40

CRIME AND JUSTICE: The Burden Study on Foundation Grantmaking Trends

This comprehensive work examines foundation funding for programs involved with crime prevention, juvenile justice, law enforcement, correction facilities, rehabilitation, and victim assistance. It looks at significant developments in the criminal justice field, changing public perceptions of crime, and cuts in governmental expenditures. It also documents the growth of funding for programs combating spouse and child abuse, and those assisting victims of violence.

April 1991/ISBN 0-87954-381-7/$35

BIBLIOGRAPHIES

THE LITERATURE OF THE NONPROFIT SECTOR: A Bibliography with Abstracts, Volumes I–IV

This bibliographical series covers references on fundraising, foundations, corporate giving, nonprofit management, and more. The entries are divided into twelve broad subject fields, and each volume includes subject, title, and author indexes. Many of the entries are abstracted to give a clear idea of the material covered in each work. Volume IV expands coverage to over 8,500 titles.

Volume IV, September 1992/ISBN 0-87954-447-3/$45
Volume III, September 1991/ISBN 0-87954-386-8/$45
Volume II, July 1990/ISBN 0-87954-343-4/$45
Volume I, August 1989/ISBN 0-87954-287-X/$55
Volumes I-IV Set/$145

SELECTED PUBLICATIONS ON NONPROFIT MANAGEMENT

THE BOARD MEMBER'S BOOK, 2nd Edition

by Brian O'Connell, President, INDEPENDENT SECTOR

Based on his extensive experience working with and on the boards of voluntary organizations, Brian O'Connell has developed this guide to the essential functions of voluntary boards. It offers practical advice on how to be a more effective board member and how board members can help their organizations make a difference.

September 1993/ISBN 0-87954-502-X/$24.95

MANAGING FOR PROFIT IN THE NONPROFIT WORLD

by Paul B. Firstenberg

Drawing upon his 14 years of experience as a professional in the nonprofit sector at the Ford Foundation, Princeton, Tulane, and Yale Universities, and Children's Television Workshop as well as his extensive for-profit experience, in this book Firstenberg outlines innovative ways in which nonprofit managers can utilize state-of-the-art management techniques developed by the most successful for-profit enterprises.

September 1986/ISBN 0-87954-159-8/$19.95

THE NONPROFIT ENTREPRENEUR: Creating Ventures to Earn Income

Edited by Edward Skloot

In a well-organized, topic-by-topic analytical approach to nonprofit venturing, Edward Skloot demonstrates how nonprofits can launch successful earned income enterprises without compromising their missions. Topics in this collection of writings include legal issues, marketing techniques, business planning, avoiding the pitfalls of venturing for smaller nonprofits, and a special section on museums and their retail operations.

September 1988/ISBN 0-87954-239-X/$19.95

A NONPROFIT ORGANIZATION OPERATING MANUAL:
Planning for Survival and Growth

by Arnold J. Olenick and Philip R. Olenick

This desk manual for nonprofit executives covers all aspects of starting and managing a nonprofit. The authors discuss legal problems, obtaining tax exemption, organizational planning and development, board relations; operational, proposal, cash, and capital budgeting; marketing, grant proposals, fundraising, and for-profit ventures; accounting, computerization, tax planning, and compliance.

March 1991/ISBN 0-87954-293-4/$29.95

PROMOTING ISSUES AND IDEAS: A Guide to Public Relations for Nonprofit Organizations

by Public Interest, Public Relations, Inc. (PIPR)

PIPR, specialists in promoting the issues and ideas of nonprofit groups, presents proven strategies, including the "nuts-and-bolts" of advertising, publicity, speechmaking, lobbying, and special events; how to write and produce informational literature that leaps off the page; public relations on a shoestring budget; how to plan and evaluate "PR" efforts, and the use of new communication technologies.

March 1987/ISBN 0-87954-192-X/$24.95

RAISE MORE MONEY FOR YOUR NONPROFIT ORGANIZATION: A Guide to Evaluating and Improving Your Fundraising

by Anne L. New

In *Raise More Money,* Anne New sets guidelines for a fundraising program that will benefit the incipient as well as the established nonprofit organization. This guidebook has three sections: "The Basics," which delineates the necessary steps a nonprofit must take before launching a development campaign; "Fundraising Methods," which encourages organizational self-analysis and points the way to an effective program involving many sources of funding; and "Fundraising Resources," a 20-page bibliography that highlights the most useful research and funding directories.

January 1991/ISBN 0-87954-388-4/$14.95

SECURING YOUR ORGANIZATION'S FUTURE: A Complete Guide to Fundraising Strategies
by Michael Seltzer

Michael Seltzer, a pioneer in the field of nonprofit management and fundraising, provides bottom-line facts and easy-to-follow worksheets to organize financial planning for beginners and a complete review of the basics plus new money-making ideas for veteran fundraisers. Seltzer's work is supplemented with an extensive bibliography of selected readings and resource organizations.

February 1987/ISBN 0-87954-190-3/$24.95

SUCCEEDING WITH CONSULTANTS: Self-Assessment for the Changing Nonprofit

Succeeding with Consultants provides practical advice for nonprofit executives eager to improve their organization's performance. Written by Barbara Kibbe and Fred Setterberg and supported by the David and Lucile Packard Foundation, this book guides nonprofits through the process of selecting and utilizing consultants to strengthen their organization's operations. The book emphasizes self-assessment tools and covers six different areas in which a nonprofit organization might benefit from a consultant's advice: governance, planning, fund development, financial management, public relations and marketing, and quality assurance.

February 1992/ISBN 0-87954-450-3/$19.95

MEMBERSHIP PROGRAM

ASSOCIATES PROGRAM

- Annual membership in the Associates Program delivers important information from:

  —foundation and corporate annual reports, brochures, press releases, grants lists, and other announcements

  —IRS 990-PF information returns for over 33,000 U.S. foundations—often the only source of information on small foundations

  —books and periodicals on the grantmaking field, including regulation and nonprofit management

- The Associates Program places this vital information at your fingertips via a *toll-free telephone number.* The annual fee of $495 for the Associates Program entitles you to *10 free calls of 15 minutes each, or 2½ hours worth of answers per month.*

- Membership in the Associates Program allows you to request *custom searches of the Foundation Center's computerized databases,* which contain information on *over 33,000* active U.S. foundations and corporate givers. There is an additional cost for this service.

- Associate Program members may request photocopies of key documents. Important information from 990-PFs, annual reports, application guidelines, and other resources can be copied and either mailed or faxed to your office. The fee for this service, available only to associate members, is $2.00 for the first page of material and $1 for each additional page. Fax service is available at an additional charge.

- All Associate Program members receive the Associates Program quarterly newsletter. It provides news and information about new foundations, changes in boards of directors, new programs and new publications from both the Foundation Center and other publishers in the field.

For more information call TOLL-FREE 800-424-9836.

FOUNDATION CENTER DATABASES

Foundation and Grants Information Online

The Foundation Center offers two important databases online. Perhaps the most flexible way to take advantage of the Foundation Center's vast resources, computer access lets you design your own search for the foundations and corporate givers most likely to support your nonprofit organization. Online retrieval provides information on funding sources, philanthropic giving, grant application guidelines, and the financial status of foundations to the following: nonprofit organizations seeking funds, grantmaking institutions, corporate contributors, researchers, journalists, and legislators.

The Center's up-to-date and authoritative data is available online through DIALOG Information Services, and through many online utilities. For further information on accessing the Center's databases directly through DIALOG, contact DIALOG at 415-858-2700.

DIALOG User Manual and Thesaurus

To facilitate your foundation and corporate giving research in these databases, the Center now offers the new *User Manual and Thesaurus*. See the ordering information described on page 174 if you are interested in obtaining the *User Manual*.

About the Authors

Jane C. Geever is president, and Patricia A. McNeill is executive vice president, of J.C. Geever, Inc., a development consulting firm in New York City founded by Ms. Geever in 1975. The firm is a longstanding member of the American Association of Fund-Raising Counsel (AAFRC).

For 18 years, J.C. Geever, Inc. has been successful in helping nonprofits to obtain funding from foundations, corporations, and individuals.

Ms. Geever is currently serving as treasurer of AAFRC and is a member of the National Society of Fund Raising Executives (NSFRE) and the Philanthropic Advisory Council for the Better Business Bureau in New York.

Ms. McNeill is a member of NSFRE and serves each year as a Mentor at Fund Raising Day in New York. She is also a member of Women in Financial Development.

Both Ms. Geever and Ms. McNeill lecture widely on subjects related to fundraising, grantsmanship, and philanthropy.

In addition to their extensive experience with proposal writing, Ms. Geever and Ms. McNeill orchestrate and render a wide array of fundraising services to diverse organizations throughout the country under the auspices of their firm.